FOUR VIEWS ON HELL

▲ ▲ ▲ ▲ ▲ ▲ ▲ ▲ ▲ ▲ ▲ ▲

FOUR VIEWS ON HELL

Edited by William Crockett

ZondervanPublishingHouse
Academic and Professional Books
Grand Rapids, Michigan

A Division of HarperCollins*Publishers*

To Karen

Four Views on Hell
Copyright © 1992 by William V. Crockett

Requests for information should be addressed to:
Zondervan Publishing House
Academic and Professional Books
Grand Rapids, Michigan 49530

Library of Congress Cataloging-in-Publication Data
    Four views on hell / William V. Crockett . . . [et al.].
       p.   cm.
    Includes bibliographical references and indexes.
     Contents: The literal view / John F. Walvoord — The metaphorical view /
William V. Crockett — The purgatorial view / Zachary J. Hayes — The
conditional view / Clark H. Pinnock.
     ISBN 0-310-53311-2
     1. Hell—Christianity.   I. Crockett, William V.
    BT836.2.F68   1992
    236'.25–dc20   92-19247
                                                CIP

Edited by Leonard G. Goss and Verlyn D. Verbrugge
Cover design by Eric Lecy
Cover illustration taken from "The Last Judgement" by Gustave Doré

Printed in the United States of America

92 93 94 95 96 97 / CH / 10 9 8 7 6 5 4 3 2 1

CONTENTS

FOREWORD

Probably the most disturbing concept in Christian tradition is the prospect that one day vast numbers of people will be consigned to hell. Almost everyone has friends or family members—people we dearly love—who are outside the faith and who, if they die in this condition, will be cast away from the presence of God. So disturbing is the idea of hell that most pastors and church members simply ignore the doctrine of final retribution, preferring to talk in vague terms about a separation of the wicked from the righteous.

But what is hell? A literal place of flame and smoke? A banishment from God? Annihilation? Is there such a place as purgatory where people are readied for the presence of God? In this book four professors describe in nontechnical language what they think the final judgment will be like, and then at the end of each chapter, they evaluate the opinions of their colleagues.

Those who have always wondered about the nature of hell will find the differing perspectives interesting and informative. Although the authors differ sharply on some points, they do so in a congenial spirit, with hope that the arguments in this book will help readers to form their own opinions. Above all, the authors agree that God is not pleased with disobedience and has appointed a day to judge the peoples of the world. Revelation 20:12 reminds us of that grave and solemn occasion with these words: "And I saw the dead, great and small, standing before the throne, and books were opened."

The Publisher

Chapter One

THE LITERAL VIEW

John F. Walvoord

THE LITERAL VIEW

John F. Walvoord

PROBLEMS IN THE CONCEPT
OF ETERNAL PUNISHMENT

Most Christians have natural problems with the concept of eternal punishment. In their study of Scripture they have been instructed from the pulpit on a loving Savior who died on the cross for our sins, rose again, and provides grace and forgiveness for all who put their trust in him. Many Christians will hear hundreds of sermons on this theme in their lifetime. On the contrary, they will probably never hear a sermon on hell, though they may hear some allusions to it from time to time. Almost immediately problems arise. What about those who live and die without ever hearing the gospel? Are they doomed to eternal punishment? Is a religious Jew or a religious Muslim who carefully follows his religion doomed to eternal punishment? How can one harmonize the concept of a loving, gracious God with a God who is righteous and unforgiving? These are very real problems that naturally call for solution.

The concept of hell as eternal punishment has long been caricatured as a relic of the Dark Ages. For many, the proper doctrine is that of a loving God who will not demand everlasting retribution. Frequently the subject is approached critically, and there is an obvious unwillingness to deal directly with the biblical evidence. In fact, some openly say that if the Bible teaches eternal punishment, they do not believe it even though it is in the Bible.

For those who believe in the genuineness of biblical revelation and accept the inerrancy of Scripture, the problem is one of understanding what Scripture teaches. Such people consider the Bible as the norm and standard for harmonizing the concept of divine, inexorable righteousness with the concept of God's infinite love. Those who deny scriptural inerrancy naturally have no problem in supporting the idea that eternal punishment does not exist. But even the most ardent advocates of eternal punishment must confess shrinking from the idea of hell as continuing forever. It is only natural to harbor the hope that such suffering may be somehow terminated. The problem for all is to comprehend the infinite righteousness of God that must judge those who have not received grace. The human mind is incapable of comprehending an infinite righteousness and must bow to the Scriptures and their interpretation when directly and faithfully set forth.

The Bible also teaches about eternal heaven; few have problems with this concept if they accept the Bible testimony. The problem is how to harmonize an eternal heaven with that of eternal punishment.

VARIOUS VIEWS

The doctrine of hell is a feature of divine revelation in Scripture and has been discussed at length in theology. The Bible clearly teaches that there is life after this life both for those who are qualified for blessing and for those qualified for judgment. The slow unfolding of this doctrine in Scripture, however, has given rise to a number of views on the subject.

First, the *orthodox* view is commonly interpreted to be the belief that punishment for the wicked is everlasting and that it is punitive, not redemptive. Because the Bible reveals that God is a God of love and grace, a tension has developed between the concepts of a loving God and of a righteous God who demands absolute justice of the wicked. It is generally conceded, however, that a strict orthodoxy provides a literal everlasting punishment for the wicked.

Second, a view of hell as *metaphorical*, that is, somewhat nonliteral and less specific than the orthodox view, has also attracted many followers. Usually it is conceded that those who are wicked will never be redeemed and restored to a place of blessing in eternity, but the scriptural accounts of their suffering and divine judgment are taken in a less-than-literal understanding.

A third view—that of the Roman Catholic Church—sees hell as *purgatorial*; that is, hell has an ante-chamber called purgatory, a place of divine cleansing from which some, at least, will eventually emerge as redeemed and be among the blessed of God. Generally speaking, this view requires that all must go through a period of purgation in which their unconfessed sins are judged and punishment inflicted. Though it may be extensive and continue over a period of time, ultimately, many will be restored to a place of grace and bliss, though others will be damned eternally.

Fourth, the view of hell as a *conditional* or temporary situation for the wicked has been advocated by many who find a contradiction between the doctrines of everlasting punishment and of a God of love and grace. As a result, they explain that hell is either temporary, in the sense that immortality is conditional and only the righteous will be raised, or that it is redemptive, in the sense that whatever suffering there may be after this life because of sin will end up in the wicked being redeemed and restored to a place of blessing. In other words, conditional immortality or annihilation lessens the severity and the extent of everlasting punishment, while in universalism, all are eventually saved.

Obviously, if hell lasts forever, these views cannot be correct, and the general tradition of the orthodox church and those who follow Scripture strictly view hell as a punishment that is everlasting for those who are not Christians or rightly related to God.

Variations in understanding the duration and extent of everlasting punishment have occupied Jewish and Christian theologians for centuries, including some Jewish theologians before the time of Christ. Some, like R. H. Savage, are even willing to deny what the Scriptures teach.

> If the doctrine of eternal punishment was clearly and unmistakably taught in every leaf of the Bible, and on every leaf of all the Bibles of all the world, I could not believe a word of it. I should appeal from these misconceptions of even the seers and the great men to the infinite and eternal

Good, who only is God, and who only on such terms could be worshiped.[1]

It is possible to provide almost endless quotations from the early Fathers up to modern theologians who believe in eternal punishment and who do not. Though a study of these opinions is informative, it really proves nothing except that there has been diversity of opinion from the beginning. However, that diversity is clearly linked to the question of whether the Bible exegetically teaches eternal punishment, and, if so, whether the Bible should be believed. Ultimately, the question is, What does the Bible teach?[2] Whole works can be found dedicated to refutation of someone who opposes eternal punishment, such as a reply to Dr. Farrar's challenge of eternal punishment.[3]

HELL IN THE OLD TESTAMENT

The Old Testament doctrine of hell unfolds slowly but surely. The principal term used to refer to life after this life is *sheol*, occurring sixty-five times in the Old Testament. Its etymology is uncertain. In the KJV it is translated "grave" thirty-one times, "hell" thirty-one times, and "pit" three times. In the NIV the usual translation is "grave."

It is clear from the Old Testament that *sheol* in many cases means no more than the grave or the place where a dead body is placed. In Psalm 49:14, for instance, the statement is made, "Like sheep they are destined for the grave, and death will feed on them. The upright will rule over them in the morning; their forms will decay in the grave, far from their princely mansions." In many other cases, however, it is debatable whether the term "grave" is a proper designation. Even the NIV translates *sheol* otherwise in Deuteronomy 32:22: "For a fire has been kindled by my wrath, one that burns to the realm of death below." The NIV tries to avoid the idea of two compartments in *sheol*. It is the mind of the interpreter that determines whether

---

[1]R. H. Savage, *Life After Death*, quoted by A. H. Strong in *Scriptural Theologies* (Philadelphia: Judson Press, 1907), 1035.

[2]For a survey of the many opinions, see Harry Buis, *The Doctrine of Eternal Punishment* (Philadelphia: Presbyterian and Reformed Publishing Company, 1957), 53–143.

[3]See E. B. Pusey, *What Is of Faith as to Eternal Punishment?* (Oxford: James Parker and Company, 1880).

sheol in a particular passage refers to the grave only or to life after this life in the intermediate state.

The uncertainty as to how *sheol* should be interpreted in the Old Testament led to the extensive debate carried on by William G. T. Shedd with Charles Hodge. Shedd's *Dogmatic Theology* debated at great length the meaning of *sheol* in his discussion on the intermediate state.[4] Shedd took the position that when *sheol* is used of the saints it refers only to the grave, but when used of the unsaved, in many instances it refers to life after death in a place of judgment and punishment. This is a debatable premise that is difficult to prove. In his discussion he opposed the mythological concept of life after death in which the place of the dead is divided into two compartments, one for the wicked and the other for the righteous. Accordingly, he opposed the teaching of some theologians that prior to the death of Christ *sheol* had two compartments, one for the lost and one for the saved (paradise), but that paradise was not equivalent to heaven. Shedd held that paradise equals heaven in the Old Testament as well as in the New Testament.

Charles Hodge, a contemporary of Shedd, did not find the two-compartment theory of *sheol* in the Old Testament incompatible with Scripture. He wrote: "Sheol is represented as the general receptacle or abode of departed spirits, who were there in a state of unconsciousness; some in a state of misery, others in a state of happiness. In all points the pagan idea of *hades* corresponds to the scriptural idea of Sheol."[5] Hodge found support in Luke 16:19–31, in the parable of Lazarus in Abraham's bosom and the rich man in *hades*.[6] The fact that the Old Testament view of *sheol* is less specific than the New Testament view of *hades* is not surprising according to Hodge: "It is not, therefore, a matter of surprise that the doctrine of the future state is much less clearly unfolded in the Old Testament than in the New. Still it is there."[7]

In any case, the Old Testament clearly teaches that there is judgment for the unsaved after this life and that this judgment continues over an extended period of time. The New Testament

---

[4]William G. T. Shedd, *Dogmatic Theology* (Charles Scribner's Sons, 1891), 2:591–640.

[5]Charles Hodge, *Systematic Theology* (New York, 1892), 3:717.

[6]Ibid., 3:725–27.

[7]Ibid., 3:715.

confirms this insofar as the unsaved are viewed as still existing at the Great White Throne Judgment—some having been in *hades* for thousands of years—but are cast into the lake of fire at that time (Rev. 20:14).

As described in the Old Testament, *sheol* is a place of darkness. Job, for instance, describes it in these words: "Before I go to the place of no return, to the land of gloom and deep shadow, to the land of deepest night, of deep shadow and disorder, where even the light is like darkness" (Job 10:21–22). The expression "silence of death" is used in Psalm 94:17 (cf. 115:17). David also questions whether there will be any praise to God from the grave (Ps. 6:5). Those in the grave have no knowledge of what is transpiring on earth. As Job states in Job 14:21, "If his sons are honored, he does not know it; if they are brought low, he does not see it." Job goes on to say that the one in the grave "feels but the pain of his own body and mourns only for himself" (14:22). The book of Ecclesiastes enlarges on this:

> Anyone who is among the living has hope—even a live dog is better off than a dead lion! For the living know that they will die, but the dead know nothing; they have no further reward, and even the memory of them is forgotten. Their love, their hate and their jealousy have long since vanished; never again will they have part in anything that happens under the sun (Eccl. 9:4–6).

The dismal picture of *sheol* in many passages of the Old Testament, however, is offset by some passages that apply blessedness for the righteous. The Old Testament clearly teaches that for the righteous, life after this life is one of blessedness, as in the case of Enoch, who went to heaven without dying (Gen. 5:24). Balaam stated in one of his oracles, "Let me die the death of the righteous, and may my end be like theirs!" (Num. 23:10). In a psalm of Asaph, the poet said, "You guide me with your counsel, and afterward you will take me into glory" (Ps. 73:24). While there are occasional references to blessedness in the intermediate state, most of the references to hope after this life for the righteous anticipate their future resurrection and blessing in the presence of God. Comparatively little is said about the intermediate state in the Old Testament.

The lot of the wicked, however, is also made clear. *Sheol* was a place of punishment and retribution. In Isaiah the

Babylonians killed in divine judgment are pictured as being greeted in *sheol* by those who died earlier. The prophet writes:

> The grave below is all astir to meet you at your coming; it rouses the spirits of the departed to greet you—all those who were leaders in the world; it makes them rise from their thrones—all those who were kings over the nations. They will all respond, they will say to you, "You also have become weak, as we are; you have become like us" (Isa. 14:9–10).

The reference in the NIV to the "grave" in verse 9 is *sheol*, though translating it this way does not explain the conscious state of those who are mentioned in the passage.

As previously mentioned, Deuteronomy 32:22 states, "For a fire has been kindled by my wrath, one that burns to the realm of death below." The "realm of death below" refers to *sheol* and implies that there is punishment by fire once an unsaved person dies. The Old Testament is clear that judgment follows the death of the wicked; see Job 21:30–34, where the idea that the wicked escape punishment and are spared from the day of calamity and God's eternal wrath is declared to be "falsehood." Obviously, the wrath of God is more than mere physical death. Psalm 94:1–2 states, "O LORD, the God who avenges, O God who avenges, shine forth. Rise up, O Judge of the earth; pay back to the proud what they deserve." In verse 23 of the same psalm the psalmist says of God, "He will repay them for their sins and destroy them for their wickedness; the LORD our God will destroy them." In Isaiah 33:14–15, Isaiah writes, "The sinners in Zion are terrified; trembling grips the godless: 'Who of us can dwell with a consuming fire? Who of us can dwell with everlasting burning?'" Of the wicked whom God will condemn, the same prophet later writes, "And they will go out and look upon the dead bodies of those who rebelled against me; their worm will not die, nor will their fire be quenched, and they will be loathsome to all mankind" (Isa. 66:24).

Though it may be conceded that the Old Testament revelation is only partial and much confirming revelation is found in the New Testament, it clearly suggests that the sufferings of the wicked continue forever. Many opponents of the concept of eternal punishment point out, however, such important words in the Old Testament as *olam* and *nesah*, though commonly translated "ever" (as in the KJV, where it is so translated 267 times), nevertheless, in some contexts is limited as to its duration in time. In Exodus 27:21 in the KJV, for example, the lamp in the tabernacle as burning always is stated to be "a statute for ever." The NIV, recognizing that the tabernacle does not continue forever, describes it as "a lasting ordinance." Furthermore, many promises in Scripture that are to be fulfilled as long as the earth lasts obviously are not forever, because the earth itself will be destroyed.

To some, that the idea of "forever" does not always mean an infinite duration in time may seem to be an unnecessary concession to the opponents of eternal punishment. But like the word "all," this word has to be interpreted in its context; and where the context itself limits the duration, this needs to be recognized in fairness to the text. At the same time, however, an important principle must be observed all throughout the Scriptures: while the term "forever" may sometimes be curtailed in duration by its context, such termination is never once mentioned in either the Old or New Testament as relating to the punishment of the wicked. Accordingly, the term continues to mean "everlasting" or "unending in its duration." Unfortunately, this is not recognized by those who are opposed to eternal punishment.

Though the total testimony of the Old Testament is somewhat obscure on details, the main facts are clear. There is life after death. The life for the righteous is blessed; the life for the wicked is one of divine judgment and punishment. There is no intimation that this punishment should not be taken literally and continue eternally. Obviously, however, much additional light is cast upon the subject in the New Testament, where the word *hades* is equivalent to the Old Testament word *sheol*.

THE INTERTESTAMENTAL PERIOD

In the last four hundred years before Christ there was extensive discussion among Jewish theologians concerning the Old Testament doctrine of everlasting punishment. Generally speaking, the Pharisees taught that there was everlasting punishment, while the school of Hillel thought that the punishment of the ungodly would last only a year before they would be annihilated. The latter believed that some of the more wicked would go on being punished for some time.[8] These interpretations of Jewish scholars in the intertestamental period are not decisive as they lack the further revelation of the New Testament. Their conclusions are not backed by Scripture.

GENERAL TEACHING OF THE NEW TESTAMENT ON HELL

In the New Testament three different words are used in regard to life after death for the unsaved. The Greek word *hades* is transliterated as "Hades" in the NIV in five instances (Matt. 16:18; Rev. 1:18; 6:8; 20:13, 14); twice it is translated as "in the depths" (Matt. 11:23; Luke 10:15), once as "hell" (Luke 16:23), and twice as "the grave" (Acts 2:27, 31). In general, the Greek word *hades* is equivalent to the Old Testament *sheol*. The same problem exists as to whether it refers only to the grave or to life after death in the intermediate state. A question can naturally be raised why the NIV, after avoiding using transliteration in all the Old Testament references of *sheol*, transliterated *hades* as "Hades" in some New Testament passages and in others used three different words where the context is hardly determinative. Be that as it may, what is clear is that *hades* is used of the temporary place of the unsaved after death but is not used in relationship to the lake of fire or eternal punishment, though it implies duration at least for the time being.

The most definitive term in the New Testament is *gehenna*, uniformly translated "hell" and referring to everlasting punishment (Matt. 5:22, 29, 30; 10:28; 18:9; 23:15, 33; Mark 9:43, 45, 47; Luke 12:5; James 3:6). One instance of the Greek word *tartaros* is found in 2 Peter 2:4; it is translated "hell" and considered equivalent to *gehenna*. It is obvious that the New Testament adds considerably to the doctrine of life after death and particularly to the subject of everlasting punishment.

THE TEACHINGS OF JESUS

One of the most significant aspects of the doctrine of everlasting punishment is the fact that Jesus himself defined this more specifically and in more instances than any New

---

[8]Cf. Harry Buis, "Hell," in *The Zondervan Pictorial Encyclopedia of the Bible*, ed. Merrill C. Tenney (Grand Rapids: Zondervan, 1975), 3:114–15.

Testament prophet. All the references to *gehenna*, except James 3:6, are from the lips of Christ himself, and there is an obvious emphasis on the punishment for the wicked after death as being everlasting. The term *gehenna* is derived from the Valley of Hinnom, traditionally considered by the Jews the place of the final punishment of the ungodly. Located just south of Jerusalem, it is referred to in Joshua 15:8 and 18:16, where this valley was considered a boundary between the tribes of Judah and Benjamin. In this place human sacrifices were offered to Molech; these altars were destroyed by Josiah (2 Kings 23:10). The valley was later declared to be "the valley of slaughter" by Jeremiah (Jer. 7:30–33). The valley was used as a burial place for criminals and for burning garbage. Whatever its historical and geographic meaning, its usage in the New Testament is clearly a reference to the everlasting state of the wicked, and this seems to be the thought in every instance. In James 3:6 the damage accomplished by an uncontrolled tongue is compared to a fire which "corrupts the whole person, sets the whole course of his life on fire, and is itself set on fire by hell."

Christ warned that a person who declares others a fool "will be in danger of the fire of hell" (Matt. 5:22). In Matthew 5:29 Christ states that it is better to lose an eye than to be thrown into *gehenna*, with a similar thought regarding it being better to lose a hand than to go into *gehenna* (Matt. 5:30). In Matthew 10:28 believers in Christ are told not to be afraid of those who kill the body, but rather to "fear him which is able to destroy both soul and body in hell" (KJV). A similar thought is mentioned in Matthew 18:9, where it is declared better "to enter life with one eye than to have two eyes and be thrown into the fire of hell." In Matthew 23:15 Christ denounces the Pharisees who "travel over land and sea to win a single convert, and when he becomes one, you make him twice as much a son of hell as you are." In Matthew 23:33 he denounces the Pharisees and the scribes, asking the question, "How will you escape being condemned to hell?" In Mark 9:43, 45, 47, the thought recorded in Matthew about it being better to lose part of the body than to be cast into hell is repeated (cf. Matt. 5:22, 29, 30). Luke 12:5 contains a similar thought to that expressed in Matthew 10:28, that one should fear the devil far more than those who might kill them physically. Though not always expressly stated, the implication is that the punishment will have duration and be endless.

Though the word *gehenna* is not used in Matthew 7:19,

some believe that this is what Christ meant when he said, "Every tree that does not bear good fruit is cut down and thrown into the fire." Also implied in Christ's statement in Matthew 7:23 is the truth that part of the punishment of hell is to be separated from Christ forever: "Then I will tell them plainly, 'I never knew you. Away from me, you evildoers!'"

In the parable of the weeds (Matt. 13:18–23) Christ declares that the weeds will be burned (Matt. 13:29), implying punishment by fire. In the parable of the talents (Matt. 25:14–30), the worthless servant is thrown "into the darkness, where there will be weeping and gnashing of teeth" (Matt. 25:30). Likewise, the goats in the revelation of the judgment of Gentiles (Matt. 25:31–46) are declared to be cast "into the eternal fire prepared for the devil and his angels" (verse 41), again implying everlasting punishment. Other instances are found, such as Matthew 18:6, where it states that it would be better to be drowned than to lead a child astray. In the parable of the wedding feast (Matt. 22:13), the one without a garment is cast "into the darkness, where there will be weeping and gnashing of teeth" (Matt. 22:13).

Jesus also indicated that punishment in hell would be by degrees, depending on their understanding of the will of their master. Accordingly, one servant would have a lighter beating than another (Luke 12:47, 48), and hypocrites would receive more condemnation than others (Mark 12:40). If one accepts the authority of Scripture as being inerrant and accurate, it is clear that Christ taught the doctrine of everlasting punishment.

According to Paul, the wicked will receive sudden destruction when the Day of the Lord overtakes them (1 Thess. 5:3) and will suffer divine wrath (1 Thess. 5:9). The punishment of the wicked is described as "everlasting destruction," which is more than physical death, and as being "shut out from the presence of the Lord and from the majesty of his power" (2 Thess. 1:9). In Hebrews 6:3 "eternal judgment" is in store for those who are unsaved, and in 10:27 this is enlarged with a reference to "only a fearful expectation of judgment and raging fire that will consume the enemies of God."

Likewise, punishment is predicted for the angels, as stated emphatically in 2 Peter 2:4: "God did not spare angels when they sinned, but sent them into hell, putting them into gloomy dungeons to be held for judgment." Angels will not be judged finally until the end of the millennium and hence will be punished for a long period of time. This is declared to be in

keeping with God's program of judging the world at the time of
Noah and condemning the cities of Sodom and Gomorrah; his
declared purpose is "to hold the unrighteous for the day of
judgment, while continuing their punishment" (2 Peter 2:9).
The reference to hell in 2 Peter 2:4 is the one instance in the
Bible where *tartaros* is used for everlasting punishment. This
word is frequently found in Jewish apocalyptic literature, where
it refers to a place even lower than hell where the wicked are
punished.

Jude adds a word of special revelation concerning the
angels as being "kept in darkness, bound with everlasting
chains for judgment on the great Day" (Jude 6). This is
compared to the judgment on the people of Sodom and
Gomorrah, who are "an example of those who suffer the
punishment of eternal fire" (Jude 7).

Revelation 14:10–11 states that those who receive the mark
of the beast, indicating worship of the final world ruler as God,
"will drink of the wine of God's fury, which has been poured
full strength into the cup of his wrath. He will be tormented
with burning sulfur in the presence of holy angels and of the
Lamb. And the smoke of their torment rises for ever and ever.
There is no rest day or night for those who worship the beast
and his image, or for anyone who receives the mark of his
name." By contrast, the martyred dead are declared to be
blessed of the Lord (Rev. 14:13–14). Though neither *hades* nor
gehenna is found in Revelation 14, the statement clearly defines
hell as eternal punishment.

While *gehenna* is not found in the book of Revelation, *hades*
is referred to in four instances (Rev. 1:18; 6:8; 20:13–14). In
Revelation 1:18 Christ is said to "hold the keys of death and of
Hades." Christ himself is described as "the Living One; I was
dead, and behold I am alive for ever and ever!" (Rev. 1:18). Just
as Christ was referring to his own physical death in this
passage, it may be assumed that the death of those for whom
he holds the key is also physical death. *Hades*, however, in
some instances refers to more than the grave and indicates the
intermediate state, as Christ himself taught in Luke 16:19–31.
In Revelation 6:8 the pale horse, representing death, is described: "Its rider was named Death, and Hades was following
close behind him." The reference may be to physical death and
the grave, or it may in the context go beyond the grave to the
intermediate state of suffering for the wicked.

Two of the most important references occur in Revelation

20:13–14, where it is stated: "The sea gave up the dead that were in it, and death and Hades gave up the dead that were in them, and each person was judged according to what he had done. Then death and Hades were thrown into the lake of fire. The lake of fire is the second death." John implies that the grave will some day give up the bodies of the wicked dead and that they will be resurrected in order to enter into the eternal punishment of the lake of fire. The fact that they are still in existence indicates that their existence was not terminated when they died physically, but they are still alive and suffering torment in *hades*, the intermediate state up to this point. This state is then emptied, however, and those who are in it are cast into the lake of fire, the second death; this action indicates eternal separation from God.

The lake of fire does not provide annihilation but continual suffering. In Revelation 20:10, when the devil is cast into the lake of fire at the end of the millennium, the beast, the world ruler, and the false prophet who were thrown into the lake of fire at the beginning of the thousand-year reign of Christ are still there, sharing torment in the lake of fire with the devil "day and night for ever and ever" (Rev. 20:10). In Revelation 21:7–8 the unsaved are pictured as having their place "in the fiery lake of burning sulfur." Though the word *gehenna* is not used, the lake of fire is, and it serves as a synonym for the eternal place of torment.

If it is conceded that the Bible clearly teaches that there is punishment after this life and that this punishment has duration, the question must now be raised whether the Scriptures clearly state that this is everlasting.

IS THE PUNISHMENT OF THE WICKED EVERLASTING?

The concept of eternity, or everlasting, is found frequently in both the Old and New Testaments. In the Old Testament a number of Hebrew words are used to express the thought of eternity, such as *olam, alam, nesah*, and *ad*. In the New Testament *aionios* is used most prominently.

As Buis points out, the Greek word *aionios* in every instance refers to eternity. He writes: "*Aionios* is used in the New Testament sixty-six times: fifty-one times of the happiness of the righteous, two times of the duration of God in His glory, six other times where there is no doubt as to its meaning being endless, and seven times of the punishment of the wicked."[9] By contrast, Buis points out that *aion* is used ninety-five times but not necessarily of unlimited duration. He states: "*Aion* is used ninety-five times: fifty times of unlimited duration, thirty-one times of duration that has limits, and nine times to denote the duration of future punishment."[10] Even *aion*, however, is sometimes used of endless punishment, as in 2 Corinthians 4:18, where the eternal is contrasted to the temporal.

In support of the idea that *aionios* means "endless" is its consistent placement alongside the duration of the life of the godly in eternity. If the state of the blessed is eternal, as expressed by this word, there is no logical reason for giving limited duration to punishment. As W. R. Inge states, "No sound Greek scholar can pretend that *aionios* means anything less than eternal."[11]

The assertion of Buis and Inge that *aionios* always means eternal is challenged by some on the basis of texts where there may be a question about it. In Romans 16:25, for instance, the word is used in regard to the "mystery hidden for long ages past" (*aionios* is translated "hidden for long ages past"). The KJV translates *aionios* with the phrase "through times eternal." Here eternity is viewed as extending from eternity in the past to the present rather than eternity beginning in the present and going on endlessly in the future. Accordingly, it may be held that Romans 16:25 regards *aionios* as having an infinite duration even though terminated in time, just as eternal punishment has eternal duration but begins in time.

Aionios also occurs in 2 Timothy 1:9, where it is translated "the beginning of time" ("before times eternal" in the KJV). Here the thought is the same: infinity extending to the past rather than to the future. In Titus 1:2 *aionios* is translated "the beginning of time" ("times eternal" in the KJV). Again the thought is the same: infinity extending to the past rather than to the future. In Philemon 15 *aionios* is translated "for good" in the NIV, but "for ever" in the KJV. Here the thought is that beginning in time Paul will have fellowship with Philemon

---

[9] Buis, *Doctrine of Eternal Punishment*, 49.

[10] Ibid., 49.

[11] W. R. Inge, *What Is Hell?* (New York: Harper and Brothers, 1930), 6; quoted by Buis in *Doctrine of Eternal Punishment*, 49–50.

forever, that is, to infinity. If understood in these ways, *aionios* is used in all these texts with an infinite sense, either to the past or to the future. In none of these cases does it simply mean "for a long time."

The concept of eternity is frequently attributed to God in the Old Testament (Ps. 10:16; 41:13; 45:6, 8; 48:14; 90:2; Isa. 9:6; 26:4; Mic. 4:7; Mal. 1:4, to name just a few of the many references). The New Testament has a similar emphasis on the eternity of God (John 8:35; 12:34; Rom. 1:25; 9:5; 2 Cor. 9:9; Heb. 5:6; 6:20; 7:17; 13:8; 2 Peter 3:18). This doctrine is especially emphasized in the book of Revelation (1:6; 4:9, 10; 5:13, 14; 7:12; 10:6; 11:15; 15:7).

A frequent use of the concept of eternity is that of eternal life attributed to those who are born again (Matt. 25:46; Mark 10:30; John 3:15; 4:36; 5:39; 6:51, 54, 58, 68; 10:28; 12:25; 17:2, 3; Acts 13:48; Rom. 2:7; 5:21; 6:23; etc.). In evangelical Christianity the eternity of God and the eternal life of those who are saved are universally recognized. The question remains as to whether this concept of eternity is carried over into eternal punishment.

In the Old Testament, where eternity is principally expressed by the Hebrew *olam*, it becomes obvious that the same word that is used of God and his eternity is also used of some promises that are fulfilled in time. For example, the promise of the land of Canaan given to Israel in Genesis 13:15, stated to be perpetual or forever, is clearly taught to be unconditional as to fulfillment but limited as far as duration is concerned. Obviously, when a new heaven and new earth are created, the land of Canaan will no longer exist as a separate entity. Likewise, the Law is referred to frequently as a statute forever (Ex. 12:24; 27:21; 28:43; etc.). But again, it was given as a temporary rule of life for Israel which is superseded in the New Testament by the age of grace, with many of the details of the Law no longer applicable. Regarding the use of the Hebrew word *olam* as the concept of eternity, therefore, each passage needs to be studied in the light of its context.

A general rule, however, can be established that unless Scripture specifically terminates a promise given "forever," limiting it to time in contrast to eternity, we may assume that "eternity" means "everlasting," as indicated in the character of God and in the character of salvation in Christ. In a similar way, "all" means "all" unless limited by the context. When examined in the light of this principle, the promises of eternal punishment have no such alleviating factor. The book of

Revelation attributes eternity to God and, at the same time, states that the wrath of God continues forever (Rev. 15:7; 19:3).

The ultimate convincing argument for eternal punishment is found in Revelation 20:10–15, in the context of how eternity will change things in time. In this passage, as has been previously pointed out, the beast and the false prophet, cast into the lake of fire at the beginning of the millennium (19:20), are still there a thousand years later and are declared to join with Satan in the torment which will continue "day and night for ever and ever" (20:10). The state of the wicked is likewise declared to be that of being cast into the lake of fire. The wicked who had suffered in *hades,* in some cases for thousands of years, are then transferred to the lake of fire (20:12–15). John goes on to imply they will have a permanent "place . . . in the fiery lake of burning sulfur" (21:8). Instead of predicting the termination of punishment, all the implications of these statements support the doctrine of eternal punishment. Finally, though *aionios* is generally used of eternal life, it is specifically coupled with punishment of the wicked in Jude 7, where Jude says of Sodom and Gomorrah: "They serve as an example of those who suffer the punishment of eternal fire." This is in contrast to "eternal life" mentioned in verse 21.

As I have said earlier, a confirmation of eternal punishment is found in the use of the Greek word *aionios.* A most convincing evidence that eternity usually means "without beginning or end" is found in the definition of this word in Arndt and Gingrich.[12] This word is used normally in the New Testament to mean either "without beginning or end" or at least "without end." None of the passages uses the word in a sense other than infinity in time, but it may mean infinity in time past or infinity in time future. The similar word, *aion,* while generally meaning "eternity," sometimes means "an age or a portion of eternity," much like *olam* in the Old Testament.

The earlier conclusion that eternal punishment is everlasting, regardless of the terminology, is supported by the fact that it is never regarded as being terminated. This holds for the New Testament especially. Doubting the matter of eternal punish-

---

[12]Walter Bauer, William F. Arndt, F. Wilbur Gingrich, and Frederick W. Danker, *Greek-English Lexicon of the New Testament* (Chicago: University of Chicago Press, 1979), 28.

ment requires either doubting the Word of God or denying its literal, normal interpretation.

CAN ETERNAL PUNISHMENT BE HARMONIZED WITH THE LOVE AND GRACE OF GOD?

Some who concede that the Bible teaches eternal punishment nevertheless say that this concept is alleviated by the fact that God is a God of love and a God of grace. As the evidence unfolds on the eternity of punishment of the lost, it becomes clear that the objections to it are not exegetical but theological. This illustrates the centuries-long tension between theology, or a system of interpretation, and biblical exegesis. If exegesis is the final factor, eternal punishment is the only proper conclusion; taken at its face value, the Bible teaches eternal punishment. This observation is supported by the fact that many who reject eternal punishment also reject the inerrancy and accuracy of the Bible and even reject the teachings of Jesus. For instance, Buis quotes Theodore Parker in his *Two Sermons*, "I believe that Jesus Christ taught eternal punishment . . . I do not accept it on His authority."[13] One is faced with the fact that the only place one can prove absolutely that God is a God of love and grace is from Scripture. If one accepts the doctrine of God's love and grace as revealed in the Bible, how can that person question, then, that the same Bible teaches eternal punishment?

The problem here is the obvious lack of understanding of the infinite nature of sin as contrasted to the infinite righteousness of God. If the slightest sin is infinite in its significance, then it also demands infinite punishment as a divine judgment. Though it is common for all Christians to wish that there were some way out of the doctrine of eternal punishment because of its inexorable and unyielding revelation of divine judgment, one must rely in Christian faith on the doctrine that God is a God of infinite righteousness as well as infinite love. While on the one hand he bestows infinite grace on those who trust him, he must, on the other hand, inflict eternal punishment on those who spurn his grace.

[13]Theodore Parker, as quoted by S. C. Bartlett in *Life and Death Eternal* (New York: American Tract Society, 1866), 148; quoted by Buis, *Doctrine of Eternal Punishment*, 34.

IS ETERNAL PUNISHMENT
TO BE UNDERSTOOD LITERALLY?

Obviously, the description of eternal punishment in the Bible only partially reveals its true nature. Eternal punishment is partly mental, partly physical, and partly emotional. The fact that confinement in hell is pictured also as a place of total darkness is no doubt contributory to mental anguish, though there is no indication of genuine repentance in hell. The emotional problems of facing eternal punishment are beyond human computation and are certainly a major portion of the judgment that is inflicted on the wicked.

IS THE FIRE OF ETERNAL PUNISHMENT TO BE UNDERSTOOD LITERALLY?

In the attempt to alleviate some of the suffering of eternal punishment, the question is naturally raised as to whether the fire of eternal punishment is literal. However, the frequent mention of fire in connection with eternal punishment supports the conclusion that this is what the Scriptures mean (cf. Matt. 5:22; 18:8–9; 25:41; Mark 9:43, 48; Luke 16:24; James 3:6; Jude 7; Rev. 20:14–15).

There is sufficient evidence that the fire is literal. In the case of the rich man and Lazarus in Luke 16:19–31, the rich man in *hades* asked father Abraham to cool his tongue with water because, "I am in agony in this fire" (v. 24). Thirst would be a natural reaction to fire, and the desire to cool his tongue would be in keeping with this description.

It is true that Scripture sometimes uses a language of appearance, describing something as nearly as possible in terms that can be understood in our present life. This acknowledgment does not alter the fact, however, that punishment is eternal and that it is painful, both mentally and physically. Scripture never challenges the concept that eternal punishment is by literal fire. Objections have to be on philosophic or theological grounds rather than on exegetical ones.

Though it may be true that the picture of eternal punishment is only a partial revelation of its true character, obviously, the reality of it is no less painful or severe. Eternal punishment is an unrelenting doctrine that faces every human being as the alternative to grace and salvation in Jesus Christ. As such, it is a spur to preaching the gospel, to witnessing for Christ, to praying for the unsaved, and to showing compassion on those who need to be snatched as brands from the burning.

Response to John F. Walvoord

William V. Crockett

Although John Walvoord argues for a fiery, eternal hell, he does so not from an uncaring spirit, but because he believes it to be the clear teaching of Scripture. In his introduction he confesses the inner hope all of us feel that somehow God may shorten the suffering of those consigned to hell. But for Walvoord this cannot be. Hell is an endless place of suffering where the wicked burn in literal fire.

I share Walvoord's view (against Pinnock) that hell in the New Testament is a place of endless conscious punishment. I also share his concern that Scripture must be our guide in any conclusions we make about the final destiny of the wicked. I differ, however, when it comes to the nature of the punishment in hell. Walvoord is mistaken when he argues that hell is a place of intense heat, material fire, and smoke akin to the fires of an earthly furnace. The writers of the New Testament were not concerned so much with the exact nature of hell as they were with the seriousness of coming judgment.

Walvoord recognizes that Scripture sometimes uses the language of appearance when describing things, but he does not think this is the case when it comes to the descriptions of hell. Why? Because the term "fire" is often used in connection with eternal punishment and because the flames mentioned in the story of the rich man and Lazarus (Luke 16:19–31) sound like literal flames. Besides, he says, Scripture never disputes that eternal punishment is by literal fire.

Trying to decide whether language in Scripture is literal or symbolic has always proven difficult. In spite of this, there is overwhelming evidence (developed more fully in my section of this book) that the New Testament pictures of hell are metaphors and not literal descriptions.

First, the biblical writers do not intend their words to be taken literally. Jude calls hell the "blackest darkness" (Jude 13) when only moments earlier in verse 7 he pictures it as an "eternal fire." The same is true for Matthew, who often uses the opposite images of fire (Matt. 3:10, 12; 25:41) and darkness (8:12; 22:13; 25:30) when describing hell. If we extend this to the broad sweep of New Testament theology, we can hardly miss the incongruent images of blackest darkness in Jude and Revelation's vast "lake of fire" (Rev. 19:20; 20:10, 14–15; 21:8).

Second, physical fire works on physical bodies with physical nerve endings, not on spirit beings. We see in Matthew 25:41 that the eternal fire was created for spirit beings like the devil and his angels. The fire must in some sense be a spiritual fire, which is another way of acknowledging it to be a metaphor for God's punishment of the wicked.

Third, the New Testament descriptions of heaven and hell are symbolic pictures, not itemized accounts of eschatological furniture. The writers use the most powerful symbols available in the first century to communicate their meaning. Heaven is pictured as an ancient city, adorned with the treasures of the world. It comes complete with golden streets, pearled gates, jewel-laden walls, and sparkling rivers. Even the most lowly have plenty of food, spacious living quarters, and eternal rest. Hell is the opposite. There the wicked suffer in darkness and fire, afflicted by maggots and tormented with blows. There they weep and gnash their teeth. Like stars, they wander in eternal night, a symbol of ultimate remorse, where joy and hope are forever lost.

Fourth, in ancient times teachers often used words symbolically to underscore their points (rabbinic hyperbole, as we now call it). To be a disciple you must "hate" your father and mother (Luke 14:26), "gouge out" an offending eye (Matt. 5:29), let the dead "bury their own dead" (Luke 9:60). Such colorful language was understood by all to be hyperbole, picturesque speech to bring home the urgency of the situation. The same is true with the images of hell recorded in the New Testament. Their purpose is not to give the reader a detailed, literal picture of torment, but a symbolic one.

Fifth, the pictures we have of hell outside the Bible in

Jewish literature are vivid and mostly symbolic. The object was to paint the most awful picture possible, no matter how incompatible the images. Writers warn of "black fire" (2 Enoch 10:2), "blazing flames worse than fire" (1 Enoch 100:9), and a place where the wicked burn eternally, even though at the same time their bodies rot with maggots (Judith 16:17; Sirach 7:17). Their picturesque descriptions are not meant to be literal reports of the doings of the damned, but warnings of coming judgment.

Walvoord thinks the wicked will be plunged into a literal abyss of fire and smoke largely because the New Testament descriptions of hell are vivid and concrete. But this is no reason to conclude that hell will be a furnace of fire. Jewish writers often painted hell in vivid and concrete pictures, even though their descriptions were substantially less than literal. For them, and for the New Testament writers, the final abode of the wicked was a place of profound sorrow, a place of ruin that words could never describe. To say that the wicked would "suffer the punishment of eternal fire" (Jude 7) is consistent with saying they will be cast into the "blackest darkness" (Jude 13). Both are metaphors for the inexpressible judgment of God.

Response to John F. Walvoord

Zachary J. Hayes

As I read Professor Walvoord's chapter, it seems to me that he operates with a distinction between theology (or a system of interpretation) and biblical exegesis, which he believes makes it possible to cut through centuries of historical diversity and to uncover for the reader the true message of the Scriptures. There is, he argues, a long-standing tension between exegesis and theology; and when exegesis itself is allowed to be the final arbiter of the meaning of the Bible, "eternal punishment is the proper conclusion" to the question discussed in this volume. Therefore, he continues, the fire involved in this eternal punishment is to be understood in a literal sense.

Since this distinction plays such a basic methodological role in the argument of the essay, it seems appropriate to reflect on it in some detail. At first the distinction between exegesis and theological system seems clear enough. At least it is clear that factors other than the biblical text enter into systematic theological thought. On the other hand, it seems to be a view common enough among biblical scholars that there might be something like pure, disinterested exegesis which, left to itself, will yield the obvious meaning of the biblical text. The issue, however, is far from clear. We need only think of the tremendous diversity of opinion among biblical scholars to recognize that something puzzling is afoot here. And this remarkable diversity, which—in principle—ought not be there, cuts across all the denominations of western Christianity. I am referring not to people who consciously think of themselves as theologians rather than as exegetes; I am referring to people who see themselves as biblical scholars and who, presumably, have not been tainted by theological systematic concerns or philosophical thought patterns that they see as alien to Scripture.

Some of the problems involved here are underscored in Walvoord's statements about the historical diversity in Christian tradition. Like the other authors in this volume, Walvoord recognizes the presence of diversity throughout the history of Christianity. Unlike the other writers, he is inclined to see this simply as a fact of history with no particular theological significance. As he states, the fact of diversity proves nothing except that there has always been diversity.

I think the fact of diversity obscures the distinction between exegesis and theology and suggests some problems that need to be addressed. As is commonly known, cynics at times refer to the Bible as a text which can be used, and in fact has been used, to "prove" anything a particular person wishes to prove. This ought to alert us to some of the problems implied in the fact of diversity. For example, does the fact of diversity indicate that no text, including that of the Bible, is self-interpreting? And in the light of this, we must ask who is to determine what is meant by following the Scriptures strictly. Furthermore, what criteria are to enter into the making of such determinations? Are such criteria suggested by the Bible itself? If so, why is there such diversity in Christian history among sincere, well-intended, intelligent people? And if not, then from where are such criteria derived?

Systematicians and historians of doctrine think that the historical fact of diversity raises questions of a nonexegetical sort. Are they, therefore, less faithful to the meaning of the Bible? It seems to me that the way one decides to deal with this fact will have a significant impact on the understanding of what it means to "follow Scripture strictly."

In my view, such questions are foundational. The answer to them may turn out to be far more important than the interpretation of particular texts or the analysis of particular statistical data. Is there really such a thing as a purely exegetical explanation of a text? Or are there other, nontextual suppositions operating in every attempted textual interpretation? And are the possible meanings of a text determined in advance by such suppositions?

What is the real difference, then, between exegesis and

biblical theology on the one hand and a more explicitly
systematic theology on the other? Is it the difference between
those who approach the Bible with no alien presuppositions
and those who approach it with such presuppositions? The
state of biblical studies hardly seems to warrant such an
understanding. Or are we dealing with the difference between
those who operate with presuppositions but are not consciously
aware of them and those who are consciously aware of their
presuppositions and attempt to deal with them more critically?
If so, the distinction between exegesis and systematic theology
becomes far less clear.

That Walvoord's own presentation is not free of nonexegetical assumptions is clear, among other instances, in the
treatment of the language of time and eternity. Students of
contemporary biblical studies are aware of the discussions of
the language of time and eternity in O. Cullmann (*Christ and
Time*, rev. ed. [Philadelphia: Westminster, 1964]) and others.
One does not have to agree with one side or the other to realize
that this language might be somewhat more complex than is
reflected in the common concept of eternity as unending time.
Nor is there a convincing reason to persuade one that such an
understanding of eternity is the proper biblical meaning of the
term in every instance. It is not, therefore, a pure, positive
exegetical datum to say that the biblical language of eternity is
equivalent to "everlasting duration." There is good reason, I
think, to see such a statement as a theological interpretation
reflecting a particular philosophical preference. And if that be
the case, the possibility of annihilation which, presumably, is
excluded by such an interpretation might in fact be consistent
with the biblical message.

Finally, while Scripture does at times use the language of
punishment (and in the most somber terms), it uses other
language as well to elicit an awareness of the negative outcome
of human life. As a student of the history of doctrine, I suspect
that the almost normative significance given to punitive language might be determined more by late medieval soteriology
than by the data of exegesis. The elaborate otherworldly
scenario developed by medieval theologians and preachers has
left a profound impression on the Christian imagination of the
West, even though we might not be explicitly aware of it. For
many of us, this sort of scenario is with us when we read the
sacred texts and conditions of what we take these texts to
mean. While the medieval scenario provides a key for our

understanding of what the righteousness of God involves, the primary source of analogies is the law court and the legal system. Judgment and punishment as acts of God on the sinner seem inevitable.

But is it necessary to think of the final negative outcome of human existence always and exclusively as the punitive action of God? Or is it possible to think of it as that painfully devastating frustration of our own existence which we are capable of bringing upon ourselves by our failure to respond to God appropriately? What could be more tragic for us than the definitive failure to find the only sort of fulfillment in which our human reality can ultimately find its rest—namely, the fulfillment which is possible only through a proper, loving relationship with God? And what could be more painful for us than the awareness that this devastating loss is our own doing?

This is all by way of saying that the case for the literal view of hell as everlasting punishment in real fire may not be quite as straightforward as it seems at first. The arguments in favor of this view, I believe, are as laden with unexpressed presuppositions as are any other attempts at interpretation. Since I am convinced that the discussion of the argument can bear little real fruit unless those presuppositions are stated and evaluated, I have attempted to make at least an initial move in that direction.

Response to John F. Walvoord

Clark H. Pinnock

John Walvoord is a friend and esteemed Christian leader who twenty years ago invited me to address the Dallas Seminary graduation. I agree with John that hell is a terrible reality into which unrepentant sinners may fall. He is also right to insist that the doctrine of hell is an integral part of Christian theology, being a subject on which our Lord and his apostles repeatedly taught. Indeed all of us in this volume agree with him about hell being an awful possibility that exists because human beings have the freedom to reject God's love for them. They have the power to decide their eternal destiny, whether in heaven or hell. At the same time, I would qualify these harsh realities with the fact that God's mercy is such that no one is predestined to hell but may voluntarily choose it, since God is not willing that any should perish but that all should come to repentance.

I agree with Walvoord too that as biblical interpreters we have no right to soften the scriptural warnings about hell but ought to take them seriously and accept them. I would also stand with him against certain of the metaphorical views of hell, suspecting that they are really efforts to lessen the gravity of the situation. For example, Crockett twice quotes Billy Graham as musing whether hellfire might not refer to a burning in our hearts for God, and one remembers that C. S. Lewis could compare being in hell to living in a dingy, grey city. Such a hell may resemble living in Chernobyl but is hardly the equivalent to *gehenna*. Walvoord and I judge such proposals as sheer speculations that cannot be considered serious interpretations of the hell that Jesus spoke about. If fire is the biblical image, something terrible must be meant by it, even if it be a metaphor. Fire by its very nature would either consume sinners thrown into it or else torture them endlessly. There is no third possibility.

My difference with Walvoord is about the nature, not the fact of hell. John takes the position that souls condemned to hell suffer everlasting physical and mental torment, similar to what Dante describes in the *Inferno*, whereas I take the position that their suffering will finally come to an end. I believe that unrepentant sinners perish, die the second death, and are finally destroyed. Though I think I make out a better case than he does, Walvoord has an advantage over me in that his view coincides, as mine does not, with the majority view of the Christian tradition on the subject. Augustine and Edwards, like Walvoord, thought of hell as a blazing inferno of actual fire. It may be an advantage to be able to stand with the tradition on this matter.

At the same time, it should be said that Walvoord does not always stand with tradition. For example, he does not hold to Augustine's view of the millennium, infant baptism, double predestination, or the sacraments. Evidently he is prepared to offer correctives when he believes tradition has gone wrong. Therefore, he is not in a position to be shocked when I claim the same liberty to revise our tradition on the nature of hell. The fact that it proved difficult to find an evangelical theologian prepared to defend hell in literalist terms for this book suggests that I am not alone in suspecting that something may have gone wrong with the tradition on this point.

What makes it particularly hard to respond to Walvoord's chapter is the brevity and superficiality of it. How should I respond to a study that does not engage many basic issues or face up to serious difficulties in the view it is defending? There is little documentation even in support of his position and none interacting with alternative interpretations of it. Therefore, I do not even know exactly what he might say on a number of key points. The best way to respond under the circumstances is (I think) for me to list some of the difficulties he neglects and leave the readers to decide whether in their opinion a view like his can resolve them.

First, Walvoord mentions that few preachers today, even in fundamentalist circles, say much in their sermons about the literal, everlasting, conscious punishment of impenitent sin-ners. Agreeing with his observation, I would offer a different explanation of this fact from his. Their reticence is not so much due to a lack of integrity in proclaiming the truth as to not having the stomach for preaching a doctrine that amounts to sadism raised to new levels of finesse. Something inside tells them, perhaps on an instinctual level, that the God and Father of our Lord Jesus Christ is not the kind of deity who tortures people (even the worst of sinners) in this way. I take the silence of the fundamentalist preachers to be testimony to their longing for a revised doctrine of the nature of hell. I would like to oblige them.

Second, Walvoord sidesteps a grotesque moral problem. He actually asks us to believe that the God who wills the salvation of the world plans to torture people endlessly in physical fire if they decline his offer of salvation. Questions leap to mind. Who would want to accept salvation from a God like that? Has Walvoord visited the burn unit in his local hospital recently? Is he not conscious of the sadism he is attributing to God's actions? I am baffled, knowing that John is a kindly man, how he can accept a view of God that makes him out to be morally worse than Hitler. Obviously Walvoord does not intend to give this impression; nevertheless, this is the impres-sion his doctrine creates.

Third, although adamant about taking biblical language literally and willing to rest his entire case on this approach to interpretation, I do not see much evidence of him taking the Bible literally. After all, symbols of perishing and dying predominate in Scripture when the subject of the destiny of the wicked is discussed, as my section shows. Walvoord even cites texts which speak of hell as death and destruction, but these do not seem to register on his mind. I guess that the traditionalist paradigm simply blocks and filters out the contrary impression these texts create when they are allowed to speak. What eloquent testimony to the power of presuppositions. How far from being consistent literalists are!

Fourth, despite problems in his own exegesis, Walvoord still has the temerity to state that a person like me who takes a different view from him must be rejecting the inerrancy of the Bible. This is an old canard and very tiresome, especially when it comes, as it inevitably does, from those whose own case from Scripture is lamentably weak. But I hope the reader is not taken in by this deception but recognizes it as a device to discount in advance what the other person is saying. The fact of the matter is that the issue concerning the nature of hell does not involve the doctrine of biblical inerrancy at all but is entirely a matter of the valid interpretation of texts and of sound theological reasoning. (How easy it is at moments like this to sympathize with liberals who complain how hard it can be to talk with certain evangelicals.)

Fifth, further in regard to literalism, Walvoord must know (but, if not Walvoord, then the reader knows) that not all Scriptures lend themselves to literal interpretation. For example, there are figures of speech, poetic passages, and apocalyptic visions. I think we have to recognize that eschatological assertions in the Bible represent, for the most part, forms of nonliteral speech and are not best understood as literal but analogical descriptions of the future.

Sixth, why does Walvoord not even consider the possible effects that believing in the immortality of souls might have upon traditional interpretations of certain biblical texts? I am not asking him to accept that this influence would be a bad thing but only that he notice and speak to the issue. I am disappointed again.

Seventh, he tries to explain the justice of everlasting torment by saying that even a small sin against Almighty God would be infinite in significance and deserving of infinite punishment. What kind of rationale is this? What kind of God is this? Is he an unjust judge? Is it not plain that sins committed in time and space cannot deserve limitless divine retribution? It worries me that John should be content with such superficial reasoning on so crucial a matter.

Eighth, he claims that belief in hell as literal fire provides us with a spur to evangelism. This just confirms my suspicion that people hold to this teaching about hell for pragmatic and not biblical reasons—hell is the ultimate big stick to threaten people with. I would turn it around the other way: It is more likely that this monstrous belief will cause many people to turn away from Christianity, that it will hurt and not help our evangelism.

In conclusion, Walvoord's view is not likely to persuade many unconvinced people unless it can be better constructed and defended. Because I doubt that it can be, I also doubt that it will be a live option for thoughtful Christians today.

Chapter Two

THE METAPHORICAL VIEW

William V. Crockett

THE METAPHORICAL VIEW

William V. Crockett

It has been a long time, maybe twenty years, since I have heard a sermon on hell. Perhaps this reflects the churches I attend, but I suspect it has more to do with a general embarrassment Christians feel when confronted with the doctrine of eternal punishment. Even among those who affirm a literal view of hell, silence is the watchword. I suppose people feel it is better to be silent than to offend. Better to teach God's truth in positive, affirming ways than to sound vengeful and uncaring.

Positive teaching, of course, is good advice. In Jesus we find someone who genuinely cares for others, who is touched by the sorrows of the people he meets. He never turns his back on the sick and lowly and always counsels kindness in the face of adversity. Yet his words also reveal a grim fate for the wicked. A large sector of people, he says, will be plunged into hell's unquenchable fires (Matt. 7:13–14; 13:42). Could such teaching be true, *literally* true? Will a portion of creation find ease in heaven, while the rest burn in fire?

Faced with such teaching, it is not hard to see why Christians shrink from discussing the doctrine of hell. Hell is like a dirty little secret that rears its nasty head at inappropriate moments. How often has someone asked—at work, during social occasions—whether we really believe in hell? Jesus believed in hell, we reply, but somehow the picture of desperate faces shrieking in a lake of fire unsettles us. Trapped,

43

we shift awkwardly on our feet and try to soften the impact of what the Bible so clearly seems to say.

Christians should never be faced with this kind of embarrassment—the Bible does not support a literal view of a burning abyss. Hellfire and brimstone are not literal depictions of hell's furnishings, but figurative expressions warning the wicked of impending doom.

My view is similar to that of John Calvin, who determined over four hundred years ago that the "eternal fire" in texts like Matthew 3:12 is better understood metaphorically: "We may conclude from many passages of Scripture, that it [eternal fire] is a metaphorical expression."[1] Shortly before Calvin, Martin Luther rejected the artists' portrayals of hell, considering them of "no value."[2] Luther could talk of a burning hell where the wicked would wish for "a little drop of water,"[3] but in the end he had no desire to press a literal interpretation: "It is not very important whether or not one pictures hell as it is commonly portrayed and described."[4] Following the Reformers, Princeton scholar Charles Hodge stated flatly: "There seems no more reason for supposing that the fire spoken of in Scripture is to be a literal fire, than that the worm that never dies is literally a worm."[5]

Today, from my own informal survey, I would guess that most evangelicals interpret hell's fires metaphorically, or at least allow for the possibility that hell might be something other than literal fire.[6] "Do not try to imagine what it is like to be in

---

[1]John Calvin, *Commentary on a Harmony of the Evangelists, Matthew, Mark, and Luke*, trans. William Pringle (Grand Rapids: Eerdmans, 1949, reprint from 1610), 200–1.

[2]Martin Luther, *Luther's Works: Lectures on the Minor Prophets, II, Jonah, Habakkuk* (St. Louis: Concordia, 1974), 19:74.

[3]Martin Luther, *Luther's Works: Commentaries on 1 Corinthians 7, 1 Corinthians 15, Lectures on 1 Timothy* (St. Louis: Concordia, 1973), 28:144–45.

[4]*Luther's Works*, 19:75.

[5]Charles Hodge, *Systematic Theology* (New York: Scribners, 1876), 3:868.

[6]The list includes Donald Carson, Millard J. Erickson, Carl F. H. Henry, Roger Nicole, Ronald Youngblood (in conversations with me), and F. F. Bruce, Billy Graham, Donald Guthrie, Kenneth Kantzer, C. S. Lewis, Leon Morris, J. I. Packer (cited in this and following notes). F. F. Bruce in his foreword to Edward W. Fudge, *The Fire that Consumes: A Biblical and Historical Study of Final Punishment* (Fallbrook, CA: Verdict, 1982), viii; Donald Guthrie, *New Testament Theology* (Downers Grove: Inter-Varsity, 1981), 887–92; C. S. Lewis, *The Problem of Pain* (New York: Macmillan, 1962), 126; Leon Morris, "Eternal Punishment,"

hell," cautions theologian J. I. Packer, ". . . the mistake is to take such pictures as physical descriptions, when in fact they are imagery symbolizing realities . . . far worse than the symbols themselves."[7] Kenneth Kantzer, a former editor of *Christianity Today*, sums up the view of many evangelicals: "The Bible makes it clear that hell is real and it's bad. But when Jesus spoke of flames . . . these are most likely figurative warnings."[8] Likewise, evangelist Billy Graham holds a metaphorical view. He comments on the image of fire: "I have often wondered if hell is a terrible burning within our hearts for God, to fellowship with God, a fire that we can never quench."[9]

Opinions on the nature of final judgment will always be with us, and it would be presumptuous to say that I know precisely what hell is going to be like. I do not, of course, and no one else does either. When it comes to the afterlife, only the dead know for sure. Yet we do have revelation from the Lord of the living and the dead, and that revelation—the Scriptures—must be our guide. If it is not, we will find ourselves at sea, driven largely by the winds of the moment.

Even so, there is the problem of interpretation. Should we take the images of heaven and hell literally, or should we see them as metaphors pointing toward real but indefinable states? To affirm the latter is to affirm the reality of heaven and hell, but a heaven and hell that is best left unspecified. The words of Jesus and the apostles tell us that the final abode of the wicked will be a place of awful reckoning, but specifically what that reckoning will be, we cannot know for certain until we pass beyond this life. But we can, I believe, rule out some interpretations and construct a strong argument for the metaphorical view.

in *Evangelical Dictionary of Theology*, ed. Walter A. Elwell (Grand Rapids: Baker, 1984), 369–70.

[7]J. I. Packer, "The Problem of Eternal Punishment," *Crux* 26 (Sept. 1990), 25.

[8]Kenneth S. Kantzer, quoted in "Revisiting the Abyss," *U.S. News & World Report* (March 25, 1991), 63.

[9]Billy Graham, "There is a Real Hell," *Decision* 25, No. 7–8 (July–August 1984), 2. Graham also asks in *The Challenge: Sermons from Madison Square Garden* (Garden City, N.Y.: Doubleday, 1969), 75: "Could it be that the fire Jesus talked about is an eternal search for God that is never quenched? That, indeed, would be hell. To be away from God forever, separated from His Presence."

GRAPHIC VIEWS OF HELL

Throughout the ages, images of hell have fascinated the church. With few exceptions the literal view of hell dominated Christian thinking from the time of Augustine (fifth century) until the Reformers (sixteenth century). Faced with imaginations that had run riot, theologians such as Luther and Calvin declined to speculate on the literal possibilities of torment. But others, caught in the vortex of history, eagerly supplied portraits detailed enough to satisfy the most morbid of God's creatures.

The Early Days. From the second to the fourth centuries, we find no uniform view on the fate of the lost, but from some Christians emerged descriptions of hell that were gruesome beyond belief. Not satisfied with the images of fire and smoke, some of the more creative pictured hell as a bizarre horror chamber. No excess or novelty escaped them. These vivid Christian portraits are similar to, and often dependent on, earlier Jewish accounts of hell.[10] In both literatures, punishment is based on a measure-for-measure principle, as in the formula, "eye for eye, tooth for tooth" (Ex. 21:24; Lev. 24:20). For Christians, Jesus' words about final judgment were significant: "For with the judgment you make you will be judged, and the measure you give will be the measure you get" (Matt. 7:2, NRSV).

In short, whatever member of the body sinned, that member would be punished more than any other in hell (at least they attempted proximate punishment). In Christian literature[11] we find blasphemers hanging by their tongues. Adulterous women who plaited their hair to entice men dangle over boiling mire by their necks or hair. Slanderers chew their tongues, hot irons burn their eyes. Other evildoers suffer in equally picturesque ways. Murderers are cast into pits filled

---

[10]Jewish literature is often more graphic than the frightful descriptions of hell found in Christian apocalypses. The rabbis speak of licentious men hanging by their genitals, women who publicly suckled their children hanging by their breasts, and those who talked during synagogue prayers having their mouths filled with hot coals. See Saul Lieberman, *Texts and Studies* (New York: KTAV, 1974), 29–56.

[11]The principal documents that describe the fate of the damned, as held by early Christians, are *The Apocalypse of Peter, The Acts of Thomas,* and *The Apocalypse of Paul.* They may be found in Edgar Hennecke, *New Testament Apocrypha,* Vol. 2, ed. W. Schneemelcher (Philadelphia: Westminster, 1965).

with venomous reptiles, and worms fill their bodies. Women who had abortions sit neck deep in the excretions of the damned. Those who chatted idly during church stand in a pool of burning sulphur and pitch. Idolaters are driven up cliffs by demons where they plunge to the rocks below, only to be driven up again. Those who turned their backs on God are turned and baked slowly in the fires of hell.

The Fourteenth Century. Italian poet Dante Alighieri fueled these early speculations with the publication of his *Divine Comedy,* a popular work that achieved a certain notoriety in western culture.[12] He imagined a place of absolute terror where the damned writhe and scream, while the blessed bask in the glory of Eternal Light. The descriptions of hell come complete with loud wails of sinners boiling in blood, terrified and naked people running from hordes of biting snakes, and lands of heavy darkness and dense fog. In Dante's hell, people must endure thick, burning smoke that chars their nostrils, and some remain forever trapped in lead cloaks, a claustrophobic nightmare.[13]

Aside from the more gruesome details of hell's pain (details, I might add, that no sane Christian affirms today), there is another odd feature worth mentioning. A number of early theologians taught that saints in heaven could see the torments of the damned. The sight of their suffering increased the pleasure of those saints because they could see divine justice in operation, making their own bliss all the sweeter by contrast.[14] Some people found support for this teaching in the parable of Dives and Lazarus (Luke 16:19–31) and in the pronouncement that those who bear the mark of the beast will be "tormented with burning sulfur in the presence of the holy angels and of the Lamb" (Rev. 14:10; cf. Isa. 66:22–24). To say that the blessed will delight in the torture of the damned is hard to imagine, especially if the damned include loved ones. But because God is just, and because all his acts reasonably should bring joy to the righteous, some Christians are still driven to the

---

[12]Dante Alighieri, *Divine Comedy,* trans. Charles Eliot Norton (Chicago: University of Chicago, 1952).

[13]Graphic descriptions of hell are not limited to Jews and Christians. The Koran talks about the damned roasting in the flames of hell (Al-Muddaththir 74:28–29) and being forced to drink scalding water and cold pus (Sad 38:57–58).

[14]Thomas Aquinas, *Summa Theologica,* Supp. to Third Part, Q. 94, art. 1, 3; cf. Augustine, *City of God,* 20.22.

conclusion that the faithful will indeed rejoice in the misery of unbelievers. One professor (in a mainline denominational seminary, as surprising as that might sound) found the logic so compelling he often said to his students, "Once we see the glory of Christ, and the hideous nature of sin as God sees it, hell will be understandable. If my own mother were being carried to the mouth of hell, I would stand and applaud."

The Eighteenth and Nineteenth Centuries. Even after the cautions of Luther and Calvin, a number of prominent preachers and theologians still expected hell to be a sea of fire where the wicked would forever burn. They interpreted the New Testament's images of hell literally and saw no need to explain them otherwise. The result was a vivid picture of hell that often went beyond the circle of the New Testament. They avoided the grisly pictures of earlier times, but not the temptation to fill in perdition's details.

In sermons about future punishment, the eighteenth-century American theologian Jonathan Edwards pictured hell as a raging furnace of fire. He imagined the wicked being cast into liquid fire that is both material and spiritual, that wholly fills body and soul.

> The body will be full of torment as full as it can hold, and every part of it shall be full of torment. They shall be in extreme pain, every joint of 'em, every nerve shall be full of inexpressible torment. They shall be tormented even to their fingers' ends. The whole body shall be full of the wrath of God. Their hearts and their bowels and their heads, their eyes and their tongues, their hands and their feet will be filled with the fierceness of God's wrath. This is taught us in many Scriptures . . . .[15]

The famous nineteenth-century British preacher Charles Spurgeon narrated the fate of the wicked this way:

> . . . in fire exactly like that which we have on earth thy body will lie, asbestos-like, forever unconsumed, all thy veins roads for the feet of Pain to travel on, every nerve a string on which the Devil shall forever play his diabolical tune of hell's unutterable lament.[16]

---

[15]Jonathan Edwards, in John Gerstner, *Jonathan Edwards on Heaven and Hell* (Grand Rapids: Baker, 1980), 56, n. 37; cf. pp. 54–55.

[16]Charles H. Spurgeon, as noted by Fred Carl Kuehner, "Heaven or Hell?" in *Fundamentals of the Faith*, ed. Carl F. H. Henry (Grand Rapids: Baker, 1975), 239.

Some theologians tried to visualize what it would be like trapped in a hell of liquid fire. "The fire shall pierce them, penetrate them," said theologian E. B. Pusey, ". . . like a molten 'lake of fire,' rolling, tossing, immersing, but not destroying."[17]

The Twentieth Century. Literalists today are usually more circumspect. They are loath to provide concrete accounts of hell or to detail its presumed sufferings. But lest we think that graphic pictures of hell are limited to the distant past, I remind you that there are still people who insist on taking the Bible's images in the most literal way. Naturally, we no longer see grotesque pictures of worms or reptiles gnawing on the rotting flesh of condemned humanity. But the furnace of fire and smoke is commonly represented. On my desk I have a copy of a large, superbly done book entitled, *Why Am I On This Earth?*[18] It is filled with attractive pictures and moving stories that powerfully bring home the gospel. Yet when it comes to the afterlife, the editors feel compelled to depict hell as literally as they can. Men and women clad in tattered clothes[19] stagger along the shore of a fiery lake. They rip at their hair. They clutch their throats. They crawl up the sides of burning rocks trying to find relief in a land where there is no relief. And overshadowing them in the darkened skies, the death skull watches, an eternal reminder of the wrath of God.

Descriptions of this sort no doubt arise from a genuine desire to jolt the complacent into repentance, and this, at least, is commendable. There is nothing wrong with using images to teach truth. After all, Jesus used the images of fire and darkness to warn the wicked of the consequences of sin. Difficulties arise only when we insist that the images reflect concrete reality.

In this chapter I want to underscore that the Scriptures do teach about a real hell, a place of frightful judgment. But precisely what it will be like, we do not know. The problem comes when we see the images in the New Testament—images

[17]An early sermon by E. B. Pusey, quoted in Geoffrey Rowell, *Hell and the Victorians: A Study of the Nineteenth-Century Theological Controversies Concerning Eternal Punishment and the Future Life* (Oxford: Clarendon, 1974), 108.

[18]*Why Am I On This Earth?*, ed. George Derksen (Winnipeg, Canada: Fleet, 1986).

[19]Ibid., 143. The wearing of clothes by the damned is a concession to modern times. Through the ages, especially in rabbinic and medieval times, the damned are pictured naked, while the righteous repose in heaven fully clothed.

that in themselves we can easily misunderstand—and then we add on a layer of our own imaginings. But how do we know that hell will conform to our imaginings? Perhaps hell will be nothing like them. By insisting on a literal interpretation, we may distort entirely what the Holy Spirit intends to say through the Scriptures. We ask ourselves how fire works on earth and then project that information on a setting where spirits exist and bodies are not consumed. We imagine a fiery lake tossing the wicked to and fro and saturating them with billows of fire washing over them, and, like Edwards and Pusey, we put into words what our minds see.

But is this what hell will be like? A place where the damned twist and shriek, their eyes bulging with fire, forever consumed by the wrath of God? If this were true, says theologian Nels Ferré, it would make Hitler "a third degree saint, and the concentration camps . . . picnic grounds."[20]

If we really think about it, a literal view of hell is not much different from the graphic views of Dante or the apocryphal writings of early Christians. Of course, no one today believes in a hell of snakes and boiling blood, but how is it different to say that sinners will roast in eternal fire? As Celsus, the second-century critic of Christianity, put it, God becomes the cosmic cook.[21]

THE SYMBOLIC USE OF WORDS

Naturally, we do not want non-Christians to reject the gospel because of a misunderstanding on hell. If the fate of the wicked is not a lake of fire but something else, then we need to make this clear. At the same time, we should not adopt a "softer" view because it sounds better or because it soothes our sensibilities. This simply undermines the authority of Scripture. Unfortunately, some people confuse a high view of Scripture with taking every word of the Bible literally. They think that whatever the Bible says must be true literally.

But this neglects the symbolic use of words, or what is

---

[20]Nels Ferré, *The Christian Understanding of God* (New York: Harper, 1951), 228; cf. "Universalism: Pro and Con," *Christianity Today* 7 (1963), 540. This comment was made in defense of universalism, a position that Ferré supports.

[21]Celsus in *Origen: Contra Celsum*, trans. Henry Chadwick (Cambridge: University Press, 1965), 5.14–15.

often called rabbinic hyperbole. Rabbis in ancient times (and this includes Jesus) often used colorful speech to bring home forcefully their points.[22] For example, when Jesus says, "If anyone comes to me and does not hate his father and mother, his wife and children . . . he cannot be my disciple" (Luke 14:26), he does not mean we must hate our parents to be proper disciples. That is a language vehicle used to convey the point that loyalty to him is supreme. We must love Jesus so much that our other loves seem like hate in comparison. The same is true with Matthew 5:29, "If your right eye causes you to sin, gouge it out and throw it away. It is better for you to lose one part of your body than for your whole body to be thrown into hell." We know Jesus did not intend people to take his words literally, because the context has to do with lust. Removing an eye—or even two eyes—will not help because even blind people lust. This is colorful speech by Jesus the rabbi; he means that sin is so serious that it is better to lose an eye than to perish in hell.

We must, of course, be careful not to read rabbinic hyperbole in places where Jesus intended his words to be taken literally. When the rich man asks what he should do to inherit eternal life, Jesus replies, "Sell everything you have and give to the poor, and you will have treasure in heaven. Then come, follow me" (Luke 18:22). Jesus did not mean, "Sell ten percent of what you have," says Bruce Metzger. "The context makes it absolutely clear that the questioner as well as the disciples, all of whom were Near Easterners, understood Jesus' words in their literal sense."[23] That is the meaning of Peter's words in verse 28, "We have left all we had to follow you!" In the context we understand that Jesus was serious about selling everything, especially since it was common in rabbinic times for people to give up all they had to follow after a master. By paying attention to the contexts, we can avoid overliteralizing on the one hand, or diluting the meaning of Scripture on the other.

Detecting hyperbole is not difficult in statements such as: "Take the plank out of your own eye" (Matt. 7:5); "It is easier for a camel to go through the eye of a needle than for a rich man

---

[22]A more complete discussion of this may be found in Bruce M. Metzger, *The New Testament: Its Background, Growth, and Content* (Nashville: Abingdon, 1965), 136–44.

[23]Metzger, *The New Testament*, 137.

to enter the kingdom of God" (Matt. 19:24); "Whatever you ask I will give you, up to half my kingdom" (Mark 6:23); "If anyone says to this mountain, 'Go, throw yourself into the sea,' . . . it will be done for him" (Mark 11:23); "Let the dead bury their own dead" (Luke 9:60). Even those holding a literal view of hell would not read these texts literally. The words seem to say one thing, but from the contexts we readily perceive them to be rabbinic hyperbole or colorful speech.

The same is true with the images of hell we find in the New Testament. Their purpose is not to give the reader a literal picture of torment, but a symbolic one. In Jewish and Greek literature we often find vivid pictures of hell, but generally they did not intend their fiery descriptions to be taken literally.[24] When Gentile converts to Christianity encountered hellfire descriptions similar to those they had grown up with, they would naturally interpret those portraits as symbols representing the wrath of God. If they were mistaken and hell was indeed a place of literal heat and smoke, one would expect to find a correction of this view somewhere in the literature of the Bible. But, of course, there is none.

In Jewish literature, vivid pictures of hell are given to show that God has ordained an end to wickedness. The writers do not intend their descriptions to be literal depictions of the fate of the damned, but rather warnings of coming judgment. In the Qumran texts, for example, mutually exclusive concepts like fire and darkness are used more to evoke a horrifying image than to describe a literal hell. The writers speak about "the shadowy place of everlasting fire" (1QS 2:8) and describe hell as "the fire of the dark regions" (1QS 4:13).[25] The same is true with 1 Enoch, which talks about "darkness . . . and burning flame" (103:7) and "blazing flames worse than fire" (100:9). Similarly, 2

[24]For discussion and bibliography, see Lattimore, who endorses the consensus of classical scholars that for the Greeks "the description of the underworld consists mainly of various poetical figures and seldom has more than a fanciful significance" (Richmond Lattimore, *Themes in Greek and Latin Epitaphs* [Urbana: University of Illinois Press, 1962], 87, n. 1). When Jewish thought is wedded to hellenistic culture, we often find Jewish writers interpreting things metaphorically, as in Aristobulus, a second-century B.C. Jewish document: e.g., God's hands (2:7–9), wisdom (5:10), the descent of God upon Sinai (2:17), and fire that "blazes without substance and consumes nothing, unless the power from God (to consume) is added to it" (2:15).

[25]Translations of Qumran material are by Geza Vermes, *The Dead Sea Scrolls in English* (Baltimore: Penguin, 1962).

Enoch 10:2 pictures hell as "black fire."[26] The Testament of Abraham 12–13 uses fire to picture the Last Judgment. There the archangel Purouel (whose name means fire) "tests the works of men through fire" (13:11). The fire that burns up the works of individuals in both the Testament of Abraham 13:12 and 1 Corinthians 3:15 is not a literal fire, but a symbol of something far greater.

Fire is often nonliteral in Jewish writings; they use colorful language to make a point. Even the Torah was said to have been written with "black fire on white fire" (Jerusalem Talmud, Shekalim 6:1, 49d), and the tree of life was described as gold-looking in "the form of fire" (2 Enoch 8:4). There are mountains of fire (Pseudo-Philo 11:5), rivers of fire (1 Enoch 17:5), thrones of fire (Apoc. Abram. 18:3), lashes of fire (T. Abram. 12:1)— even angels and demons of fire (2 Bar. 21:6; T. of Sol. 1:10). In the Scriptures God is said to be a "consuming fire" (Deut. 4:24), who has a throne "flaming with fire" that has a "river of fire" issuing from beneath the throne (Dan. 7:9–10). Sometimes the images of fire approximate our understanding of material fire on earth. God speaks out of fire that does not consume a desert bush (Ex. 3:1–6) and carries a prophet to heaven in a chariot of fire (2 Kings 2:11). In the New Testament, John says of the exalted Christ, "his eyes were like blazing fire" (Rev. 1:14). Fire is also used figuratively for discord (Luke 12:49), judgment (1 Cor. 3:15), sexual desire (1 Cor. 7:9), and unruly words (James 3:5–6).

As we can see, fire in Jewish and early Christian writings is regularly used to create a mood of seriousness or reverence, often having little to do with the material world of intense heat. When the writers use fire to describe judgment or hell, they use a convenient image that will demonstrate the burning wrath of God. If we try to squeeze images that were meant to be symbolic into literal molds, we ill-serve the cause of Christ. Far from helping, our fanciful theories about roaring flames awaiting unbelievers at the end of the road simply hinder the gospel. Why? Because we either say nothing about the coming judgment or offend the very people we are trying to reach.

In the first century the image of hellfire was common and

---

[26]Translations of Pseudepigraphic materials are from James Charlesworth, ed., *The Old Testament Pseudepigrapha*, Vol. 1 (Garden City, N.Y.: Doubleday, 1983).

understandable. Most people saw the fiery abyss as a symbol of something awful and indescribable. Some might have thought the fires were literal, but neither this view nor the use of fiery images created problems in antiquity. Now it is the reverse. Many in Christendom are repulsed by the message that God will consign part of his creation to a lake of fire—and they are not loath to tell us so. And what happens? We hold our tongues in embarrassment, never mentioning that God will banish the wicked from his presence. Even Hollywood, with its movies like *Ghost*, has a stronger message of coming judgment than most preachers in the pulpits of America.

The point is we must get back to preaching the whole counsel of God, and this includes warning the wicked of impending judgment. What good does it do to stand within the four walls of our churches, affirming a belief in literal flames, when outside the silence of our lips belies our very words? It is true that hell is *pictured* as a flaming pit, but this we shall see, is just that—a picture used to demonstrate the utter seriousness of divine judgment. It is simply unwarranted to describe hell in the detail given above.

And herein lies the problem of the literal view: In its desire to be faithful to the Bible, it makes the Bible say too much. The truth is we do not know what kind of punishment will be meted out to the wicked. Our responsibility is to preach and teach what we know, not to go beyond the information revealed in Scripture. God has declined to tell us everything about existence beyond the grave, but he expects us to proclaim what he has revealed. The doctrine of eternal punishment will never embarrass us when we preach what we know: Judgment is coming; flee the wrath of God. There is nothing here to feed the dark fantasies of twisted minds. What God has decided, he will do, and the nature of his judgment we leave in his sovereign hands. But if we insist on making explicit what God has deliberately left open, we become like ancient Egyptian topographers of the underworld—drawing maps of places we know nothing about.

THE METAPHORICAL VIEW

In teaching, as in preaching, concrete images are preferable to abstract allusions. Pictures bring home the point. That is why conceptual references to heaven and hell have little impact. To assure someone that righteous living will blossom in bountiful blessings may be alliterative, but is not nearly as effective as saying that one day Christians will walk streets of gold or that God will wipe all tears from their eyes. These are images that bring comfort in the bleak moments of life.

Put differently, we must be careful not to confuse the vehicle that brings truth with the message. As we saw, people in the first century often used hyperbole, or colorful language, to bring truth home. So also with the images used to describe heaven and hell: Vivid, everyday language of the first century is used to communicate the joys and sorrows of these two ultimate destinations.

Heaven. When we examine the description of heaven, we find it pictured the way we would expect first-century people to picture it (how else would they describe the heavenly city but in terms familiar to them?). Until the time of gunpowder, cities were surrounded with thick walls and sturdy gates, and inscriptions were commonly placed on or over the gates. So in Revelation we find "a great, high wall with twelve gates" (21:12), and the thickness of the walls were vast, measuring about two hundred feet (v. 17). Of course, there would be no need in heaven to have walls, but that is the way it is pictured nonetheless. On the gates were inscribed "the names of the twelve tribes of Israel" (v. 12), and on the foundations were "the names of the twelve apostles of the Lamb" (v. 14). The walls themselves were made of jasper and were built on a foundation "decorated with every kind of precious stone" (v. 19). Twelve of these precious stones are mentioned: jasper, sapphire, chalcedony, emerald, sardonyx, carnelian, chrysolite, beryl, topaz, chrysoprase, jacinth, and amethyst (vv. 19–20). "Each gate," we are told, was "made of a single pearl" (v. 21), and "the great street of the city was of pure gold, like transparent glass" (v. 21).

Today we would never describe a great city—like Paris, for example—as having walls and gates. But they would in antiquity; every city they ever knew had walls. To demonstrate that the eternal city has no need of protection, the writer pictures the gates as continually open (v. 25); and since it is a perfect city, its dimensions form a perfect cube (vv. 16–17). The city's beauty is described in many ways. Every conceivable precious stone is used in building the heavenly city, with the more valuable ones listed. Yet the stone we now cherish the most—the diamond—is absent. No doubt diamonds were overlooked because, while they were known in ancient times, they were little used. The hard carbon was simply too difficult to cut and polish. Platinum also is omitted; it was unknown until the sixteenth century.[27] Pearls, on the other hand, were among the most important adornments in antiquity. These were worn on the red sandals of Roman senators—the so-called masters of the world. But one day, says John, the most lowly of God's servants will rest in the shadow of massive gates constructed from a single pearl.

Heaven also is described as a place of rest (Heb. 3–4). Today, in the age of meaningful employment and leisure time activities, eternal rest might sound insignificant (what will we do up there?), but when people worked from dawn till dusk simply to feed themselves, the image of eternal sabbaths struck a responsive chord. Laborers in Jesus' day never took rest for granted, nor did they assume daily bread was their rightful due. (We in the West have so much food the task is how to avoid it.) So to announce that the endless delights of heaven would begin with a sumptuous feast (Rev. 19:6–9) was a picture of inexpressible happiness. Similarly, what could be more meaningful to people living in dark, one-room houses than to describe heaven as a place filled with light and space (John 14:2; Rev. 21:10–27)? Heaven was the fulfillment of every dream. The kings of this earth might possess a few trinkets of gold, but one day the faithful will walk on golden streets so wondrous that the light of heaven will shine through the gold as if it were glass. The saints, we are told, will drink from a sparkling river and eat from the tree of life that bears twelve kinds of fruit and produces leaves that heal the nations (Rev. 22:1–3).

Does this sound like a literal place? Or does God communicate truth to people in ways they can understand at their particular time in history? The apostle Paul thinks of the coming

---

[27]The twelve foundations stones in Rev. 21:9–21 are based on (though not identical with) the earlier list of twelve stones adorning Aaron's breastplate (Exod. 28:17–21). We should not think the stones are meant to be literal. Actually, the most precious are missing: ". . . the ancients, lacking modern mineralogical methods, distinguished stones largely by color. Thus, what we know as several different species were often thought to be one species. For example, the name *sapphire* referred to a blue stone, possibly *lapis lazuli*; *ruby* was probably red *spinel* or *garnet*; *emerald* most likely was *chrysoprase* (green *chalcedony*) or green *garnet*; and *topaz* was either the yellow *peridot* variety chrysolite or citrine *quartz*" (see *Lexicon Universal Encyclopedia*, ed. Sal J. Foderaro [New York: Lexicon Pub., 1987], 296.

world as entirely different from the present: "For this world in its present form (*skema*) is passing away" (1 Cor. 7:31). When discussing the resurrection body he again stresses how different heavenly things will be from what we see on earth (1 Cor. 15:35–49). And he realizes that the world above is cloaked in obscurity: "For now we see in a mirror, dimly (*ainigmati*), but then we will see face to face" (1 Cor. 13:12, NRSV). The word Paul uses for "dim" is *ainigma*, the same word we use for enigma or riddle. For Paul, the things of heaven are a riddle; he sees them, but only dimly.

C. H. Dodd suggests that Paul "shared with many of his contemporaries the belief that . . . the material universe would be transfigured into a substance consisting of pure light or glory, thus returning to its original perfection as created by God."[28] Even the possibility of such a transfiguration should caution us not to set our minds too firmly on a material heaven that parallels earth. Heaven is not earth dressed in its Sunday best; it is quite different.

In Revelation, John's vision is symbolic, but the intent is clear. Heaven is the perfect state where there is no need for the sun or moon to shine, for the radiance of God will fill the city (Rev. 21:23–24). Heaven, it turns out, is beyond our wildest imaginings, our fondest dreams. To describe it we must think of the most beautiful things on earth and multiply them a hundredfold, and still we cannot begin to grasp its beauty. "No eye has seen, no ear has heard, no mind has conceived what God has prepared for those who love him" (1 Cor. 2:9).

Hell. If heaven is described in the most powerful images available to people of that day, the same is true with hell, only with reverse implications. The images we find are shocking, and again the intent is clear. Hell is a place of profound misery where the wicked are banished from the presence of God.

In the New Testament the final destination of the wicked is pictured as a place of blazing sulfur, where the burning smoke ascends forever. This would have been an effective image

---

[28]C. H. Dodd, *The Epistle to the Romans* (London: Hodder and Stoughton, 1932), 134. See further Robin Scroggs, *The Last Adam: A Study in Pauline Anthropology* (Philadelphia: Fortress, 1966), 56, where he comments on the rabbis' belief of a restoration of the original light created on the first day. T. W. Manson, *On Paul and John: Some Selected Theological Themes*, SBT 38 (London: SCM, 1963), 26, writes: "Some transformation of the existing world seems to be implied in 1 Cor. 7:31: 'For the form of this world is passing away.'"

because sulfur fires were part of life for those who lived in the Jerusalem of Bible times. Southwest of the city was the Valley of Hinnom, an area that had a long history of desecration. The steep gorge was once used to burn children in sacrifice to the Ammonite god Molech (2 Kings 23:10; Jer. 7:31; 32:35). Jeremiah denounced such practices by saying that Hinnom Valley would become the valley of God's judgment, a place of slaughter (Jer. 7:32; 19:5–7). As the years passed, a sense of foreboding hung over the valley. People began to burn their garbage and offal there, using sulfur, the flammable substance we now use in matches and gunpowder. Eventually, the Hebrew name *ge-hinnom* (canyon of Hinnom) evolved into *geenna* (*gehenna*), the familiar Greek word for hell (Matt. 5:22, 29; 10:28; 18:9; 23:33; Mark 9:43, 45; Luke 12:5). Thus when the Jews talked about punishment in the next life, what better image could they use than the smoldering valley they called *gehenna*?

In the intertestamental period, *gehenna* was widely used as a metaphor for hell, the place of eternal damnation.[29] Later, in rabbinic literature, we find *gehenna* given a location—in the depths of the earth, and sometimes in Africa beyond the Mountains of Darkness.[30] Some Jews, of course, took the fiery images literally, supposing that Hinnom Valley itself would become the place of hellfire and judgment (1 Enoch 27:1–2; 54:1–6; 56:3–4; 90:26–28; 4 Ezra 7:36).[31] But this view was minor and not widely held in Judaism. The New Testament also rejects this view, saying that *gehenna* is already in some sense prepared elsewhere (Matt. 25:41), just as heaven is (Matt. 25:34; John 14:2; Heb. 11:16).

When Jesus talks about hell, he often uses *gehenna* and the hellenistic term *hades* (Matt. 11:23; 16:18; Luke 10:15; 16:23) to dramatize hell's suffering. Behind these two words is the image of fire, a picture often used to describe hell in antiquity. In Matthew 13:49–50 Jesus talks about the Last Judgment:

> This is how it will be at the end of the age. The angels will come and separate the wicked from the righteous and throw

---

[29] Werner E. Lemke, "Gehenna," in *Harper's Bible Dictionary*, ed. Paul J. Achtemeier (San Francisco: Harper & Row, 1985), 335.

[30] Lieberman, *Texts and Studies*, 236–39.

[31] See Hans Bietenhard, "Hell," in *The New International Dictionary of New Testament Theology*, ed. Colin Brown (Grand Rapids: Zondervan, 1976), 2:208.

them into the fiery furnace, where there will be weeping and
gnashing of teeth.

Again, in Revelation, we find at the conclusion of the Great
White Throne Judgment: "If anyone's name was not found
written in the book of life, he was thrown into the lake of fire"
(20:15). Should we take these words as indicating a literal, fiery
abyss? Or as a severe, though unspecified judgment awaiting
the wicked?

The strongest reason for taking them as metaphors is the
conflicting language used in the New Testament to describe
hell. How could hell be literal fire when it is also described as
darkness (Matt. 8:12; 22:13; 25:30; 2 Peter 2:17; Jude 14)? Those
who raise this question have a good point. Fire and darkness
are mutually exclusive terms, but as we have seen, they are
often juxtaposed in Jewish writings (Qumran, 1QS 2:8; 4:13; 1
Enoch 103:7; 2 Enoch 10:2; Jerusalem Talmud, Shekalim 6:1,
49d). The point is that when it comes to God's wrath at the end
of time, Jewish writers are not concerned with seeming
conflicts; they can describe punishment in many ways because
they have no clear scheme as to what form it will take. For
example, they often talk of hell as a place where the bodies of
the wicked burn eternally, even though at the same time they
are said to be rotting away with worms and maggots (Judith
16:17; Sirach 7:17; cf. Isa. 66:24).[32] The author of 2 Enoch 10:2
even links "black fire" with "cold ice" in the place of eternal
torment. What these writers are trying to do is paint the most
awful picture of hell they can, no matter how incompatible the
images might be. Yet of this they are certain: God will forever
punish those who walk in the paths of wickedness.

With this being said, let us ask the more pertinent
question: Did the New Testament writers intend their words to
be taken literally? Certainly, Jude did not. He describes hell as
"eternal fire" in verse 7, and then further depicts it as the
"blackest darkness" (*zophos tou skotous*) in verse 13. A similar
thing could be said for Matthew when we compare "fire" (3:10,
12; 5:22; 7:19; 13:40, 42, 50; 18:8–9; 25:41) with "darkness" (8:12;
22:13; 25:30). Moreover, a combination of fire and darkness is
complicated by the encompassing picture of a "lake of fire"
(Rev. 19:20; 20:10, 14, 15; 21:8). The blackest darkness is hardly

---

[32]Cf. Haim Z'ew Hirschberg, "Eschatology," *Encyclopaedia Judaica*, 6:875.

compatible with a vast lake of fire. From this point alone we would do well to refrain from depicting hell as a literal fire.

Fire and darkness, of course, are not the only images we have of hell in the New Testament. The wicked are said to weep and gnash their teeth (Matt. 8:12; 13:42; 22:13; 24:51; 25:30; Luke 13:28), their worm never dies (Mark 9:48), and they are beaten with many blows (Luke 12:47). No one thinks hell will involve actual beatings or is a place where the maggots of the dead achieve immortality. Equally, no one thinks that gnashing teeth is anything other than an image of hell's grim reality. In the past some have wondered about people who enter hell toothless. How will they grind their teeth? In 1950, Professor Coleman-Norton at Princeton University tried to provide an answer to this momentous question in an article entitled, "An Amusing *Agraphon*."[33] He claimed to have found, in a Morocco mosque during the Second World War, a Greek fragment containing Matthew 24:51, "there will be weeping and gnashing of teeth." When one of the disciples asks how this can be for those without teeth, Jesus replies, "Teeth will be provided." "However amusing one may regard this account," comments Bruce Metzger, "there is no doubt at all that the agraphon is a forgery." Before the war, says Metzger, Coleman-Norton often told the story "about dentures being provided in the next world so that all the damned might be able to weep and gnash their teeth."[34]

Questions about whether the damned will have literal teeth or about worms and beatings are, of course, quite useless. The apostle Paul grew impatient with similar questions from opponents at Corinth (1 Cor. 15:35–38). Not believing in the resurrection of the body, these opponents mocked the tiny Christian community and demanded to know what kind of body Christians expected to get in heaven. Paul replied in the strongest way possible, saying in effect: Anyone who asks such a question is an utter fool (*aphron*). The point is that God does what he pleases, and it does not please God to provide endless details to satisfy the curious or the argumentative. People in the

---

[33]Paul R. Coleman-Norton, "An Amusing *Agraphon*," *Catholic Biblical Quarterly* 12 (1950), 439–49.

[34]Bruce M. Metzger, "Literary Forgeries and Canonical Pseudepigrapha," *Journal of Biblical Literature* 91 (1972), 3.

next life will have spiritual bodies quite different from their present earthly ones (Acts 24:15; 1 Cor. 15:35–50).

And this raises a further question. The eternal fire was created for spirit beings such as the devil and his angels (Matt. 25:41). How then will people with spirit bodies (and disembodied spirits such as demons) be affected by a physical fire? Physical fire works on physical bodies with physical nerve endings, not on spirit beings. Perhaps the fire is in some sense a spiritual fire. This gets us back to Billy Graham's comment that hell might be better understood as a terrible eternal burning within the hearts of the lost for God, a fire that can never be quenched.

When we take into account the various images that describe hell and couple them with what seems unequivocally to be metaphorical language used for heaven, we see that God has not given us a complete picture of the afterlife. As always, God communicates to people in ways they can understand. He uses the language and images of the day to disclose truth. It comes as no surprise, therefore, to find heaven described as an ancient city, adorned with the treasures of the world. Similarly, it is quite natural for Jewish people to use regional designations like *gehenna* when referring to final punishment.

Hell, then, should not be pictured as an inferno belching fire like Nebuchadnezzar's fiery furnace. The most we can say is that the rebellious will be cast from the presence of God, without any hope of restoration. Like Adam and Eve they will be driven away, but this time into "eternal night," where joy and hope are forever lost.

ANNIHILATION OF THE WICKED

To conclude, as I have above, that the wicked will be forever banished from the presence of God is somber indeed. Whatever their punishment, wherever they are sent, the final judgment cannot be anything but laden with sorrow. Even if we were to adopt C. S. Lewis's position that hell contains relative pleasures for the damned, still, hell would rank as the worst possible place—beyond our darkest imaginings. Lewis has suggested that pleasure in hell might not be so out of line with Christian tradition as we might think.

> Even if it were possible that the experience . . . of the lost contained no pain and much pleasure, still, that black

pleasure would be such as to send any soul, not already damned, flying to its prayers in nightmare terror.[35]

What Lewis is talking about is the pain of missing heaven, or in the language of medieval scholastics, *poena damni*. This kind of torment comes not from active punishment inflicted by God— like flames scorching the skin—but from having no contact with the One who is the source of all peace. On the Judgment Day the wicked are separated from the righteous like chaff from grain, and they are carried far from the beauty and glory of God into a land of shadows where they contemplate what might have been. They are in the true sense of the word, lost forever. "Sad, sad, that bitter wail," says the hymnwriter, "Almost, but lost."[36]

Because the idea of a never-ending punishment is so harsh, even in Lewis's form, a number of evangelicals have called for a reconsideration of the doctrine. In its place they have proposed that we embrace conditional immortality or, as it is often called, annihilationism.[37] This view can be structured in many ways, but the essential point is that the wicked pass out of existence rather than endure eternal, conscious punishment in the next life.

It is common to condemn proponents of annihilationism by linking them with sects that believe in the extinction of the wicked after death, like Jehovah's Witnesses and Christadelphians. If some evangelicals are beginning to deny the existence of hell, they are probably no better than the cults, or so the reasoning goes. The parallel is interesting but says little. After all, even false prophets teach some truth; that is what makes them deceptive. The question is whether the particular doctrine at issue—annihilationism—is faithful to the Scriptures.

One caution is perhaps warranted. When someone proposes to change a doctrine taught consistently since the

---

[35]Lewis, *The Problem of Pain*, 126.

[36]Philip P. Bliss, in the song "Almost Persuaded."

[37]John Wenham, "The Case for Conditional Immortality," at the Edinburgh, Scotland conference, August, 1991, examining "Universalism and the Doctrine of Hell" by John R. W. Stott, in David L. Edwards and John R. W. Stott, *Evangelical Essentials: A Liberal-Evangelical Dialogue* (Downers Grove: InterVarsity, 1988), 306–31; see also Philip E. Hughes, *The True Image: The Origin and Destiny of Man in Christ* (Grand Rapids: Eerdmans, 1989), 398–407; Clark H. Pinnock, "Fire, Then Nothing," *Christianity Today* 31 (1987), 40–41; Fudge, *Fire That Consumes*.

inception of the church, it should make us wonder how everyone throughout the centuries could have been so terribly wrong. Not that an error could not have been made or that traditions are infallible. They are not, of course. In fact, the position I hold, suggesting a metaphorical understanding of hell rather than a place of literal heat and smoke, should raise similar caution. Actually, it has been advocated only since the sixteenth century. The true test is how well the view conforms with the biblical data.

The Problem of Harmony. As I have said, the significant point of the annihilationist view is that the wicked will not endure an eternal hell; they will simply be extinguished. If this were not so, say the annihilationists, how could there be harmony in the cosmos? When God creates a new heaven and a new earth (Isa. 65:17; Rom. 8:19–23), is it not reasonable to expect the whole creation to be at peace with God? If somewhere, in some dark corner of the universe, there are still rebellious or suffering creatures gnashing their teeth, how can this be considered harmony?

This is a reasonable argument, but an argument that better suits universalism than it does annihilationism. The logic of harmony at the end of time would suggest that God will gather *all* his creation into one big harmonious family, rather than setting up a cosmic scaffold on the Judgment Day to dispatch masses of people into oblivion.

In any case, the problem with this kind of argument is that it imposes present-day expectations on ancient writers. The annihilationists suppose that a new heaven and a new earth should produce harmony, or else the renovation is somehow incomplete. To annihilationists it seems ludicrous to say that God will renovate nature, yet still have sinners languishing in hell. But the Jewish writers of late antiquity do not follow this line of reasoning. It matters little whether the wicked are destroyed, plunged into hell, or otherwise shriveled into insignificance. They never suggest that harmony must come from annihilation as opposed to eternal suffering. Put bluntly, harmony comes when evil is removed—notwithstanding the method. To them the wicked are hostile elements, intrusions that mar the landscape of God's renovation. When judgment finally comes, the wicked are cast aside, and that is all that matters.

The writer of 2 Baruch is typical: "The coming world will be given to these [the righteous], but the habitation of the many others will be in the fire" (44:15). Later he becomes more specific, saying that the souls of the wicked will shrivel into "horrible shapes" and "will waste away even more. . . . then they will go away to be tormented" (51:5–6). The righteous, on the other hand, are "full of joy" (14:13) in anticipation of being changed "into the splendor of angels" (51:5).

At Qumran the sect members can talk about eternal punishment and annihilation at the same time, leaving today's readers to ponder their view on the fate of the wicked:

> . . . everlasting damnation by the avenging wrath of the fury of God, eternal torment and endless disgrace together with shameful extinction in the fire of the dark regions (1QS 4:12–13).

Without elaborating, it is sufficient to say that concerning the time of the renovation, the standard belief in all sectors of Judaism was that harmony would come when the perpetrators of wickedness were punished, whether by annihilation or eternal torment. To them, harmony came with the removal of the wicked. Today's annihilationists might not think the cosmos could be harmonious with the existence of hell, but this was of no concern to the ancient Jews. If the question of harmony was a non-issue in Judaism, it is likely that the same was true for the biblical writers. They could easily have held to an eternal, conscious hell with no thought that such a belief would mar the harmony of the final cosmos.

Second-Century Christians. We now turn to the question of what Scripture writers thought about the fate of the wicked. Did they assume that an evil life ended in annihilation, or in eternal, conscious suffering? An examination of the background literature surrounding the Bible is of limited help because Jewish writings contain texts that support both annihilationism[38] and eternal torment.[39] But which line do the biblical writers observe?

---

[38]Psalms of Solomon 3:11–12; *Sibylline Oracles* 4:175–85; 4 Ezra 7:61; *Pseudo-Philo* 16:3. Other presumed annihilation texts may be found in Fudge, *The Fire That Consumes*, 125–54.

[39]Judith 16:17; 1 Enoch 27:2; 53:1–3; 91:9; 2 Enoch 40:12–13; 10:1–6; *Sibylline Oracles* 52:290–310; 2 Baruch 44:12–15; 51–56; *Testament of the Twelve Patriarchs*, "Reuben" 5:5; "Gad" 7:5; "Benjamin" 7:5; *Jubilees* 36:10; 4 Maccabees 12:12. Other texts referring to eternal punishment and annihilation can be found in Emil Schürer, *The History of the Jewish People in the Age of Jesus Christ (175 B.C.–A.D. 135)*, rev. & ed. Geza Vermes, Pergus Millar, Matthew Black (Edinburgh: T. & T. Clark, 1979), 2:545.

One way of approaching this question is to examine what Christians believed at the close of the New Testament period. If these second-century Christians held consistently to one view or the other, we could reasonably conclude that the same view would have been espoused a generation or two earlier by New Testament writers.

In fact, the testimony in the first half of the second century is consistent concerning the destiny of the wicked. During the time of the early Apostolic Fathers, Christians believed hell would be a place of eternal, conscious punishment. In Ignatius of Antioch's letter *To the Ephesians* (ca. A.D. 117) we read: "Such a one shall go in his foulness to the unquenchable fire" (16:2). Likewise, in the *Epistle to Diognetus* (ca. A.D. 138) we read:

> . . . when you fear the death which is real, which is kept for those that shall be condemned to the everlasting fire, which shall punish up to the end those that were delivered to it. Then you will marvel at those who endure for the sake of righteousness the fire which is for a season (10:7–8).[40]

And *2 Clement* reads (ca. A.D. 150):

> Nothing shall rescue us from eternal punishment, if we neglect his commandments (6:7).

And again:

> . . . when they see those who have done amiss, and denied Jesus by word or deed, are punished with terrible torture in unquenchable fire (17:7).

Finally, in the *Martyrdom of Polycarp* (ca. A.D. 156–60) we read:

> And the fire of their cruel torturers had no heat for them, for they set before their eyes an escape from the fire which is everlasting and is never quenched (2:3).

And again:

> You threaten with the fire that burns for a time, and is quickly quenched, for you do not know the fire which awaits

---

[40]There is some debate regarding the dating of *Diognetus*. I assume it was written during the time of Hadrian, A.D. 117–38. See Johannes Quasten, *Patrology: The Beginnings of Patristic Literature* (Westminster, Md.: Christian Classics, 1983, orig. pub., 1950), 1:248–49.

the wicked in the judgment to come and in everlasting punishment (11:2).[41]

Unfortunately, even these texts do not seem sufficient to convince annihilationists that early Christians assumed that endless punishment would fall on the wicked. Annihilationists often construct awkward scenarios where the wicked are consumed but the fire burns forever, or where the wicked suffer greatly but temporarily in an unquenchable fire. To solve a problem they construct a fire that rages on endlessly, even though the wicked would have been consumed during the first moments of eternity. Is this what the second-century writers were trying to say? That the wicked will be destroyed in eternal, indestructible fires? Or were they following that line of thought that speaks of eternal, conscious punishment for the wicked?

It seems to me that some annihilationists look for any straw in the wind to keep from admitting that early Christians affirmed eternal, conscious punishment. Yet during the same period as Ignatius's *Ephesians* and other writings such as *Diognetus*, *2 Clement*, and *Polycarp*, we have clear testimony in another document, the *Apocalypse of Peter*, that a segment of Christian society did indeed hold to an eternal hell of suffering. This work, alluded to at the outset of this chapter, talks about gnashing of teeth and death by devouring fire (even though the wicked often suffer fates unrelated to burning). The *Apocalypse* might be faulted for its grisly details of hell's agony, with blasphemers hanging by their tongues—and other horrors— but it certainly has nothing to do with annihilation. The wicked suffer consciously and eternally (chap. 6).

I have separated the *Apocalypse of Peter* from what is usually called the Apostolic Fathers because it belongs to a body of literature known as apocryphal apocalypses. Nevertheless, it is important because it was written somewhere between A.D. 125 and 150, was held in high esteem, and was considered by many to be part of the New Testament canon.[42] Moreover, it is only one of many Christian apocalypses that insist on an eternal hell

---

[41]Translations of *Ignatius, Diognetus, 2 Clement,* and *Polycarp* are by Kirsopp Lake, *Apostolic Fathers,* Vols. 1 and 2, Loeb Classical Library (Cambridge, Mass.: Harvard University Press, 1912–13).

[42]Some rejected it, but both Clement of Alexandria (c. 150–215) and the oldest canon list of the New Testament, the Muratorian Fragment (c. 200), regarded it as Scripture. See Quasten, *Patrology, 1:144.*

of conscious suffering.[43] There can be no doubt that early in the second century, Christians believed in an eternal, conscious hell, and it would be reasonable to conclude that Ignatius's *Ephesians*, as well as *Diognetus*, *2 Clement*, and *Polycarp*, are further examples of this belief. Not much more than a generation after the writing of Matthew and Revelation, with their dire warnings to the wicked, we find not annihilation but an eternal hell, as the accepted belief for the punishment of the ungodly.[44]

If the dominant view of Christians a generation after the New Testament was eternal suffering, what possibly could have altered their supposed annihilationism? Jewish influences? Hellenistic encroachments? With respect to Jewish influences, we know that the rabbis, with few exceptions, believed hell was eternal torment.[45] But influences of this sort are exceedingly difficult to evaluate; some think Christian apocalyptic theology influenced the Jewish.[46] Whatever the case, it would be odd for second-century Christians to abandon so quickly the supposed annihilationist teachings of Christ and the apostles.

Hellenistic encroachments are often suggested as the reason for the post–New Testament church's belief in eternal suffering. Annihilationists sometimes argue that after the New Testament, Greek influences of *hades* and the immortality of the soul crept into the church. Edward Fudge writes:

> Many Christian writers of the second and third centuries . . . wrapped their understanding of Scripture in the robes of philosophy. Paul had often warned against contemporary philosophy (1 Cor. 1:19–2:5; Col. 2:1–10), but these apologists, zealous for their new-found faith, set out to battle the pagan thinkers on their own turf.[47]

---

[43]See Martha Himmelfarb, *Tours of Hell: An Apocalyptic Form in Jewish and Christian Literature* (Philadelphia: University of Pennsylvania, 1983).

[44]At the close of the second century, Christians in Alexandria reacted against eternal, conscious punishment by suggesting that the punishment in hell would eventually end. Hell was a remedial process, designed to bring fallen creatures back to God (Clement of Alexandria, *Paedogogus* 1.8; *Protrepticus* 9; *Stromata* 6.6; Origen, *De Principiis* 1.6.2–4; *Contra Celsum* 5.15 and 6.25). The point is that Clement and Origen react against the eternal, conscious suffering taught by Christians, not annihilationism.

[45]Schürer, *Jewish People in the Age of Jesus Christ*, 2:545, n. 110.

[46]See the discussion in Himmelfarb, *Tours of Hell*, 127–44.

[47]Fudge, *The Fire That Consumes*, 66–67.

There is no doubt that second-century Christian apologists
drew heavily on Greek philosophy, especially on the philosophy of the Cynics, to support the Christian position. But Fudge
makes it sound as if we have a struggle between Paul, the
Hebraic-minded Jew, and post–New Testament hellenists. In
fact, Paul himself was heavily influenced by hellenism,[48] as was
every Jew in Palestine during the first century. "In Hellenistic-
Roman times," says Martin Hengel, "Jerusalem was an 'international city,' in which representatives of the Diaspora
throughout the world met together."[49] In short, says Hengel,
"*Palestinian Judaism must be regarded as Hellenistic Judaism.*"[50] We
need to be careful, therefore, not to suggest that the New
Testament writers looked through Jewish Old Testament eyes
when in fact their literature, education, culture, philosophy,
and language were thoroughly permeated with Greek thought.

First-century Pharisees. Too often annihilationists minimize
the extent of hellenization during the first century. They think
the second-century movement of Christians toward the Greek
doctrine of the immortal soul began only after the New
Testament was written. But already in the first century we
know that the Pharisees—of which Paul was one—had ab-
sorbed the doctrine of immortality. Josephus comments on the
Pharisees:

> They believe that souls have power to survive death and that
> there are rewards and punishments under the earth for those
> who have led lives of virtue or vice: eternal imprisonment is
> the lot of evil souls, while the good souls receive an easy
> passage to a new life (*Antiquities* 8.14).[51]

> Every soul, they maintain, is imperishable, but the soul of
> the good alone passes into another body, while the souls of
> the wicked suffer eternal punishment (*War* 2.163).[52]

[48]See Robert M. Grant, "Hellenistic Elements in I Corinthians," in Allen P.
Wikgren, ed., *Early Christian Origins* (Chicago: Quadrangle Books, 1960), 60–66.
[49]Martin Hengel, *Judaism and Hellenism*, trans. John Bowden (Philadelphia:
Fortress, 1974), 252.
[50]Hengel, *Judaism and Hellenism*, 252, cf. 103–6.
[51]Josephus sometimes presents Jewish religious views in hellenistic dress
because he was writing to a Greco-Roman audience. His substance, however,
usually represents the situation accurately. See Schürer, *Jewish People in the Age
of Jesus Christ*, 2:392–93.
[52]Translation of *Antiquities* is by Louis H. Feldman in *Josephus* (Cambridge,
Mass.: Harvard University Press, 1981) and *War* is by H. St. J. Thackeray,
Josephus (Cambridge, Mass.: Harvard University Press, 1976). In addition to the

We cannot say that New Testament writers endorsed the Platonic or Pharisaic belief in a never-dying soul. If this were the case, annihilationism as a view would be impossible to maintain because the soul in every human would simply exist forever, whether in heaven or in hell. In the New Testament, however, we find the Hebrew belief in the resurrection of the dead rather than the Greek immortality of the soul (1 Cor. 15:53–55; cf. Dan. 12:2). The Pharisees believed in the resurrection as well, but only for the righteous; yet they still expected the souls of the wicked to be punished eternally. Their view combined the Greek idea of immortality with the Hebrew doctrine of resurrection.

The apostles taught that everyone, whether good or evil, would be resurrected (John 5:29; Acts 24:15; cf. Dan. 12:2); they did not suggest the soul had some special substance that made it eternal. Yet it is clear from the New Testament that both the righteous and the wicked are destined to exist forever—even though the precise nature of the resurrected bodies is not always clear. All things depend on God for their existence, and it is God who resurrects and sustains his creatures, some unto life in heaven, and some unto death—in the place we call hell.

It is important to remember that the largest and most popular group of Jews in first-century Palestine were Pharisees[53]—and they taught the imperishability of the soul. So when Jesus warns about the coming destruction in the afterlife, he does so to a Pharisaic audience. We ask ourselves, therefore, what the Pharisaic crowds would think Jesus meant when he said, "Do not be afraid of those who kill the body and after that can do no more. But I will show you whom you should fear: Fear him who, after the killing of the body, has power to throw you into hell" (Luke 12:4–5). Matthew 10:28 puts it differently: "Be afraid of the One who can destroy both soul and body in hell." These words meant something to the hearers. Would they really have been thinking that destruction in hell meant annihilation when they thought in terms of imperishable souls?

Pharisees, the Essene wing of first-century Judaism may also have believed in the immortality of the soul. For discussion, see Schürer, *Jewish People in the Age of Jesus Christ*, 2:574, and Hengel, *Judaism and Hellenism*, 198. The immortality of the soul is also taught in the second-century B.C. book *Jubilees* 23:31, and the first-century A.D. book Wisdom of Solomon 3:1–4.

[53]Schürer, *Jewish People in the Age of Jesus Christ*, 402.

And would Jesus have been so sloppy, here and elsewhere, that he never quite got his meaning across?

The point is that the imagery of hellfire must be interpreted in light of the hellenism of the first century. It is not enough for annihilationists to argue from the Old Testament (which they think has no concept of unending punishment for the wicked) to the New Testament (in which they conclude the same). Nor is it wise to import wholesale the contexts of the Old Testament into the New. For example, just because the undying worm in Isaiah 66:24 feeds on dead bodies is insufficient reason to say that the undying worm image in Mark 9:48 must relate to dead (annihilated) creatures. About 150 B.C. the Jewish composer of Judith (16:17) uses Isaiah's worm image to say that the wicked will suffer *eternal* pain. From the first century on, the fire and worms of Isaiah are commonly placed in hell, inflicting pain on the wicked who suffer eternally.[54] The important thing in interpreting any ancient text is to give proper weight to the meaning of words in the time period in which they are used.

Thus the Pharisees can be strong supporters of the Old Testament, but still embrace eternal, conscious punishment. The Christians in the early second century also can have a high view of the Old Testament, but ardently preach eternal, conscious suffering.[55]

Hell in Scripture. Before we discuss texts supporting eternal, conscious suffering, a word needs to be said about interpretation. The problem is that texts can be interpreted in many ways, as the various positions in this book amply show. Also, evidence for the correct position is never one hundred percent on one side and zero on the other. There must always be some reason for a conclusion, or nobody would be foolish enough to believe it. But we should be wary of arguments that rely on what is *possible*, rather than what is probable in light of the evidence. The people who wrote the New Testament used ordinary language and images of the first century to communicate their message, and they never expected scholars thousands of years later to be looking for *possible* interpretations. True,

---

[54]The texts may be found in Himmelfarb, *Tours of Hell,*109–10, 146–47, 160.

[55]This is not to say that the Old Testament has no concept of a resurrection of the wicked. Dan. 12:2 says, "Multitudes who sleep in the dust of the earth will awake: some to everlasting life, others to shame and everlasting contempt" (cf. Isa. 26:19). The Pharisees may have been influenced by both the Old Testament and Greek thought.

sometimes their message was misunderstood (1 Cor. 5:9–13), but it usually came across reasonably clear. So our task is to determine the everyday perspective concerning the fate of the wicked during the first century.

When we read about the plight of the rich man in hell (Luke 16:19–31), we find a typical Jewish text with strong hellenistic flavorings. The imagery of the beggar, Lazarus, resting with Abraham in heaven, while the rich man suffers in a "place of torment," conforms well with a hell of conscious suffering, and it would be understood as such by all. There is no thought of annihilation here, but a place of punishment. Of course, the Greek word used in Luke 16 is *hades*, and in Christian tradition, *hades* will be thrown into the lake of fire (Rev. 20:13–14), a euphemism for *gehenna*. For evangelical annihilationists this means that the wicked will suffer in *hades* for a season, and then destruction will follow in the lake of fire.

It is quite a large step, I think, for annihilationists to concede that there will be a temporary hell where suffering takes place. (Of course, it is almost impossible to understand the story in any other way.) It would be much cleaner for annihilationists to call the Lazarus story a parable that has no relation to reality. They could then have some kind of soul sleep for the wicked, followed by judgment and finally extermination. As it is, a temporary hell lessens annihilationism's moral argument somewhat that God is a loving God who would never put people in a place of torment. I suppose they could respond that a thousand years (or even ten thousand) in a short-term hell can never be compared to eternal pain. This has merit, but a hell of punishment—albeit temporary—does show the awful nature of sin from God's point of view. Both traditionalists and annihilationists would agree that arrogant sin is so offensive to the Creator that he consigns rebellious sinners to an intermediate hell of suffering (*hades*) that lasts in some cases thousands of years. The question is how we should take *gehenna* (the lake of fire). Is it a place of extended suffering or annihilation?

There is no doubt that the New Testament writers expected extended suffering to take place in the next age. We saw that in Mark's use of the worm image of Isaiah 66:24:

> And if your eye causes you to sin, pluck it out. It is better for you to enter the kingdom of God with one eye than to have two eyes and be thrown into hell [*gehenna*], where "their

worm does not die, and the fire is not quenched" (Mark 9:47–48).

The phrase "it is better for you" reads like Jesus' comment about Judas, "Woe to that man who betrays the Son of Man! It would be better for him if he had not been born" (Matt. 26:24). There is something about the fate of evildoers that is worse than death. In the first century, that "fate" was well understood: They called it *gehenna*, the second death. And just as the worms devoured rotting flesh in the physical Valley of Gehenna, so will they be present metaphorically in the eternal *gehenna*, where they will not die and where the fire is not quenched. This might be an odd image for us today, and we might be tempted to twist it in a number of directions, but the meaning for first-century people was clear. In hellenistic times it referred to suffering in hell. As Martha Himmelfarb says in her impressive study of apocalyptic texts, "At the beginning of the common era the fire and worms of Isaiah have been unambiguously placed in hell."[56]

In another text, Matthew 13:49–50, Jesus says:

> This is how it will be at the end of the age. The angels will come out and separate the wicked from the righteous and throw them into the fiery furnace, where there will be weeping and gnashing of teeth.

The image of the wicked weeping and gnashing their teeth is common in the New Testament (Matt. 8:12; 13:42, 50; 22:13; 24:51; 25:30; Luke 13:28). What is not common is the interpretation placed on these texts by the annihilationists. They think the agony depicted occurs shortly before the wicked are extinguished. Sometimes they point to Psalm 112:10: "The wicked man will see and be vexed, he will gnash his teeth and waste away," as if this verse has something to do with the "fiery furnace" in Matthew where "there will be weeping and gnashing of teeth." The people listening to Jesus, and later reading the New Testament record of his sayings, were well acquainted with the idea of a fiery hell. They used the word *hades*, with all its hellenistic implications, for the intermediate state, and the smoldering Gehenna Valley to represent the eternal hell. When they heard about gnashing of teeth in the fiery furnace, they quite naturally thought about eternal, conscious punishment, since that was the usual teaching of the

---

[56]Himmelfarb, *Tours of Hell*, 109.

day. Less than two generations after Matthew's gospel, the Christian *Sibylline Oracles* (ca. A.D. 150) talk about the wicked in *gehenna* gnashing their teeth and calling out for death, but death will not come (2:290–310). If Matthew had wanted his readers to understand that gnashing of teeth in the furnace of fire was annihilation, he would have had to explain this to his audience or risk being misunderstood.

There is another troubling aspect of annihilationism. The view does not adequately address the New Testament texts that talk about gradations of punishment in hell.

> That servant who knows his master's will and does not get ready or does not do what his master wants will be beaten with many blows. But the one who does not know and does things deserving punishment will be beaten with few blows (Luke 12:47–48).

Again:

> But I tell you that it will be more bearable for Sodom on the day of judgment than for you (Matt 11:24; cf. Rev. 20:11–12).

The Pharisaic-minded crowds, who believed in eternal suffering for the wicked, could not mistake what Jesus meant. Even the most vile people, he was saying, would receive a lesser sentence in the afterlife than they who had received and rejected so much truth. In other words, what you sow, you reap. If you are exceedingly evil, you will be punished exceedingly; if your sin is less, your punishment will be less when God sentences you on the Judgment Day. Annihilationism fits rather awkwardly here. It has no sense of distributive justice—Heinrich Himmler and Mahatma Ghandi receive the same punishment.

Annihilationists might respond that certain evildoers will simply suffer longer, or more intensely, before being extinguished. The problem is that the setting for the gradations of punishment in Luke 12:47–48 is *gehenna* (12:5). So now we have extended suffering in the final abode of the wicked. If we were to ask which line of Jewish eschatological punishment this fits better with—annihilationism or eternal, conscious suffering—the answer would surely be the latter. The truth is that when punishment is administered according to the depth of sin, the presumption is that the wicked will suffer for an extended time—presumably forever. For example, in the *Sibylline Oracles* noted above (2:290–310), the wicked must pay "threefold" for the evil deeds they have committed. The more evil committed, the more suffering in the next life. And their anguish in *gehenna* never ends. This is precisely the point mentioned in Matthew and Luke sixty years or so earlier. Hell is a dreadful place, but not a place of equal suffering. Some will receive lesser punishment, some more.

If gradations of punishment assume extended suffering in *gehenna*—probably endless suffering—the next two texts underscore the eternal nature of the sinner's fate.

> Then they will go away to eternal punishment, but the righteous to eternal life (Matt. 25:46).

> He will punish those who do not know God and do not obey the gospel of our Lord Jesus. They will be punished with everlasting destruction and shut out from the presence of the Lord and from the majesty of his power (2 Thess. 1:8–9).

I have already shown that the dominant view among Christians in the early second century was eternal, conscious torment. Eternal torment was also the belief held by the popular party of the Pharisees in the first century. It is into this context that the above two sayings come. When annihilationists confront these texts, they often suggest ingenious linguistic solutions which, at best, fall prey to what J. I. Packer calls "avalanche-dodging."[57]

Naturally, when we interpret a verse, the object is not to wring out every *possible* meaning and then choose one that best fits our view. The object is to see how a word or phrase is used in its literary and historical context. Before we encounter Matthew's record that the wicked will receive eternal punishment while the righteous receive eternal life, we have his discussion of gradations of punishment in hell and his sixfold warning that those who persist in evil will weep and gnash their teeth in the furnace of fire. Surely eternal punishment is balanced with eternal life: the wicked will suffer eternally, according to the extent of their sin; the righteous receive eternal life.[58]

---

[57]Packer, "The Problem of Eternal Punishment," 24.

[58]For an exegetical discussion of Matt. 25:46, see Scot McKnight, "Eternal Consequences or Eternal Consciousness," in *Through No Fault of Their Own?: The Fate of Those Who Have Never Heard*, ed. William V. Crockett and James G. Sigountos (Grand Rapids: Baker, 1991), 147–57.

Turning to Paul, when he says that the wicked will be "punished with everlasting destruction," we ask what the normal meaning would have been for him and his readers. Paul, as a former Pharisee, would have believed in eternal, conscious torment for the souls of the wicked. Luke reports that Paul the Christian expected the wicked to receive a resurrected body (Acts 24:15), so if he retained something of his Pharisaic belief, he thought the wicked would be given resurrected bodies fitted for their sojourn in hell.

But perhaps Paul no longer held the Pharisaic belief in conscious suffering for the wicked. In this case we should find some evidence somewhere to show either that he abandoned his old belief or that he had taken on a new-found understanding that evildoers would be annihilated. As it is, he speaks just as if he had never abandoned his old view. He tells people on the Greek mainland, who no doubt were heavily influenced by ideas of the immortal soul, that the wicked will be punished with *olethron aionion* (eternal destruction). When we find similar expressions elsewhere (4 Macc. 9:9; 10:15; cf. Jubilees 36:10), they mean eternal destruction in a hell of conscious suffering.

Finally, in Revelation 14:10–11 we find a deeply disturbing picture of one who rejects God. "He will be tormented with burning sulfur in the presence of the holy angels and of the Lamb." John continues, stressing that the damned will suffer eternal, conscious torment: "And the smoke of their torment rises for ever and ever. There is no rest day or night for those who worship the beast and his image." The book of Revelation has many images and symbols that should not be taken literally, but the intention in this passage is clear. The damned will suffer eternally and consciously. They will have no rest, day or night. As God "lives for ever and ever" (4:9), so will the damned suffer "for ever and ever" (14:11).

Annihilationists often suggest that John meant there will be no rest and much suffering "while it continues."[59] The phrase "for ever and ever" refers to the smoke image, a silent witness to the power of God's judgment on the wicked: they are extinguished, never to rise again. But is this what the normal reader at the close of the first century would think when reading these words? When I hear explanations of this sort, I begin to wonder how any document in antiquity could be said to endorse eternal, conscious torment. Again, when one

---

[59]Fudge, *The Fire That Consumes*, 300.

examines a passage, the question is not whether an interpretation is *possible*; it is whether it is *probable* in the context. Here John says that "the smoke of their torment rises for ever and ever. There is no rest day or night." If we were to ask what tradition Revelation follows, annihilationism or conscious suffering, the answer again can only be the latter.

Later in the book of Revelation, John describes the Holy City and the glory awaiting believers.

> The throne of God and of the Lamb will be in the city, and his servants will serve him. . . . They will not need the light of a lamp or the light of the sun, for the Lord God will give them light. And they will reign for ever and ever (Rev. 22:3–5).

Shortly after this John mentions those who are outside the city, banished from the presence of God in the place he calls the lake of fire. "Outside are the dogs," he says, "those who practice magic arts, the sexually immoral, the murderers, the idolaters and everyone who loves and practices falsehood" (22:15). These evildoers still exist, still suffer somewhere "outside" the gates of heaven. John calls the place of murderers, sorcerers, and idolaters, "the lake that burns with fire and sulfur, which is the second death" (21:8, NRSV).

The images of heaven and hell are not to be taken literally, as if there were real gates of pearl and material smoke and flames. The writers use common, everyday images to impress on their readers the reality of the next age. Heaven and hell are real; one a place of immeasurable happiness, the other of profound misery.

Response to William V. Crockett

John F. Walvoord

The statement of the metaphorical view being considered here is obviously a scholarly treatment, presented with unusual skill. It would be difficult to present this point of view more lucidly. The presentation, however, illustrates the problem that is inherent in this approach.

In studying the doctrine for myself, I soon determined that the issues could not be settled by citing authorities outside the Bible. A large bibliography only illustrates wide differences of opinion. Obviously, the world rejects the doctrine of hell, the Bible, and Jesus Christ as Savior. Even within Christian circles scholars are at odds on this important subject. The differences are not cosmetic but intrinsic in the nature of the doctrine being considered. Important premises which must be considered are: 1. Is biblical revelation without error in all its statements of fact? 2. Were the writers of Scripture influenced by the beliefs of their own generation? 3. Is prophecy to be interpreted literally? and 4. Are the theological conclusions properly based on accurate exegesis of Scripture in which all pertinent facts are considered carefully? Obviously, the answers to these questions largely determine what one concludes about the doctrine of hell.

The Metaphorical View Raises Questions about the Accuracy and Inerrancy of Scripture. The metaphorical view, as presented here, assumes that the scriptural revelation concerning hell cannot be interpreted literally. The concept of eternal hellfire is too abhorrent and, for many, too contrary to a revelation of a God of love and grace. If, as a matter of fact, hell is not described accurately in Scripture, does this not raise the question whether it is possible that the Holy Spirit was influenced in inspiring the Scriptures by the views of its human authors? In particular, was Christ himself influenced by the culture of his day, so that he taught a doctrine of hell that emphasized more than any other writer both the element of hellfire and the element of eternity? If these concepts are granted credence, does it not question both the accuracy of Scriptures and the veracity and integrity of Christ?

In trying to determine what life is like after this life, one is shut up to the Scriptures, as there is no other statement that is worthy of belief. If the Bible describes this afterlife, as far as the lost are concerned, as a place of unending punishment characterized by fire, are we free to question it? And if so, on what basis? Though the accuracy of scriptural revelation has often been questioned in modern times on the basis that it was written in a different culture and a different time and, therefore, has to be revamped to fit our current situation, the idea that the Bible is antiquated and out of date leads to total rejection of the accuracy of biblical revelation for today.

The Metaphorical View Requires a Nonliteral Interpretation of Prophecy. Probably the crux of the matter is whether prophecy should be interpreted literally. The metaphorical interpretation presented here is more conservative than some because it implies that there is retributive punishment in hell, even though it is left undefined. Furthermore, punishment is said to be eternal, which is often denied by those who adopt a metaphorical interpretation. In other words, literal fire is denied, but the fire is interpreted to represent physical and mental anguish. After all, in Scripture hell is not represented as an air-conditioned country club.

Though many scholars who interpret the description of hell metaphorically question the accuracy and veracity of Scripture, there are some who, while accepting the concept of scriptural inerrancy, nevertheless do not interpret prophecy literally. Probably the majority of the church today follows the amillennial view of prophecy which, in its most conservative statement, recognizes a literal coming of Christ but questions the severity of the tribulation that precedes as well as the literalness of a millennial kingdom that follows. If prophecy cannot be interpreted literally, as they believe, it raises important questions about the literalness of hell itself and, in large measure, determines the view of eternal punishment that an individual may take.

Those who accept a literal view of hell do so largely because they accept a literal view of prophecy. In my own studies I have published an exposition of every prophecy of the Bible. In this exercise I discovered that half the prophecies have already been fulfilled very literally. In fact, it is difficult to find a single fulfilled prophecy that was fulfilled in other than a literal fashion. Would not this historical fact require the interpretation of the future as being fulfilled literally?

The nonliteral interpretation of prophecy is largely motivated by the fact that people do not want to accept what the Bible teaches about the future, especially the doctrine of punishment—whether in this life or in the life to come. Yet the Bible records historically how God drastically punishes people because of sin, as illustrated in the history of Israel both in the destruction of Jerusalem in 586 B.C. when thousands were slaughtered, and in the destruction of Jerusalem in A.D. 70 when hundreds of thousands perished and the city was destroyed. How can a loving God destroy Israel?

This opens the larger question of how a loving God can allow earthquakes, plagues, war, and other disasters which destroy millions. Is not God sovereign? Those who are disturbed by the doctrine of hell do not face the fact that God has demonstrated in history that he can drastically destroy wicked humans. The question how a loving God can require eternal punishment of the wicked must be seen in the light of his historic judgments upon sin.

The main argument against accepting literally the doctrine of hell is that the idea of eternal punishment by fire is repulsive to many people. Granting that this is the case, are we free to interpret a Scripture in a way other than its literal meaning simply because we do not like what it says? In the history of prophecy many have questioned whether God would really judge in keeping with his warnings, only to have these prophecies literally fulfilled.

The Metaphorical View Lacks Proper Exegesis that Includes All the Pertinent Facts Relating to this Doctrine. I find it singular that this very carefully drawn chapter does practically nothing with the doctrine of sin and its infinite character in relation to the infinite righteousness of God. It hardly mentions the righteousness of God and the necessity of punishment. It assumes that the symbolic view of hell is justified on the basis of human objections to a literal view. As stated, however, the metaphorical view does allow for eternal punishment, though the author offers very little proof and no exegesis of the terms for eternity that are found in the Bible. Mention is made of apparent suffering in *hades* now, but there is no recognition of the fact that some in *hades* have been there for thousands of years and, apparently, for that period have been suffering and will continue to suffer up to the time they are cast into the lake of fire (Rev. 20).

If the view be adopted that hellfire is not literal, what is the nature of punishment in hell? The most prominent description of both hell and the lake of fire (including *gehenna*) is the characterization that it is fire. If, for the sake of argument, fire be considered symbolically, of what is it a symbol? The rich man in *hades* is said to be in "agony" (NIV), in "torment" (NASB), or in "torments" (KJV). This describes *hades* as it exists today. According to Revelation 20:10, the devil, the beast, and the false prophet will "be tormented day and night for ever and ever" (NIV, NASB, KJV). This describes the future lake of fire. Not much is gained by taking the fire of hell as symbolic, thus softening the punishment of either *hades* or the lake of fire.

One searches in vain in this chapter for an exegesis of Revelation 20:10, one of the most illuminating texts in the Bible on the subject of the duration of punishment. This text makes clear that the beast and the false prophet will be cast into the lake of fire at the time of the Second Coming but before the thousand-year reign of Christ. After a thousand years in this situation, when the devil is cast into the lake of fire also, the beast and the false prophet are still there and still being tormented, and the sweeping statement is made, "They will be tormented day and night for ever and ever." There is not a single passage in the Bible that ever states that the punishments of hell are temporary or will be terminated. Obviously, when it refers to destruction, it refers to destruction of the body and the resulting judgment of God that occurs at death.

It is obvious that arguments for a literal view of hell fall on deaf ears largely because those who hear do not want to hear. They find it impossible to reconcile this concept with their idea of a loving God who is indulgent and forgiving. However, the Bible makes plain that while God exercises grace to those who put their trust in Christ, there is no grace for anyone outside of Christ. The fallen angels were never offered grace, even though they sinned only once, and those in life who do not avail themselves of grace, for whatever reason, are revealed to be headed for eternal punishment. I would join with others who wish that the situation were otherwise and that some termination of suffering and some alleviation of the punishment might be discovered, but I cannot find it in the Bible.

Response to William V. Crockett

Zachary J. Hayes

I read Professor Crockett's essay on the metaphorical understanding of the biblical imagery for hell with a feeling of being quite close to home theologically. I welcome his historical background study for at least some degree of metaphorical interpretation, since this helps dissipate the fear that such an approach to Scripture is nothing but a "modernistic" watering down of the biblical message, one that might be suspect because it could seem to be rooted in suspicious anthropological concerns. In fact, the awareness of the presence of analogy, symbol, metaphor, and story in the Scriptures was around long before any such thing as an Enlightenment humanism saw the light of day. Certainly one would be slow to accuse Luther or Calvin of such modernistic dilution. Placing the issue of language in such a historical context makes it clear that the question is not one of modern versus traditional views. Nor is it a question of Protestant versus Roman Catholic views. Rather, the concern about the nature of biblical language cuts across the ages as well as across denominations. This, I think, is an important insight; for it suggests helpful ways of evaluating the differences of interpretation not only in the past but in the present as well.

At the heart of Crockett's argument is the conviction that it is perfectly possible to be serious about the reality of hell and yet be convinced that the language with which the Scriptures and the tradition speak about this reality is the language of imagination and that of positivistic logic. The argument moves

from the conviction brought home to many of us in the late
1960s, namely, that the "medium" is not necessarily identical
with the "message." In this case, to speak of metaphor in itself
is to make no judgment about the reality or unreality of the
object spoken about. It is merely to name a style of speech.
Metaphor is simply a way of attempting to communicate a
particular "message"; it is not itself the message. And, conceiv-
ably, there may be other ways of speaking of the message. I feel
completely at home with this perspective. To me it seems in
harmony with the ancient practice of allegorization which, as I
understand it, was basic not only in the early church fathers,
but even played a significant role in the composition of the
Bible itself.

When pushed, I might even be tempted to argue that this
approach to the text might qualify as the most literal approach.
If by literal we mean to take the text for what it really is, would
this not mean that we read a poem as a poem, a fable as a fable,
a piece of historical narrative as history, etc? Specifically, would
it not mean that we read metaphors literally for what they are
when we read them precisely as metaphors and not as actual
descriptions of fact? The question then becomes how to
recognize when we are dealing with metaphors and when we
are not. With reference to eschatology, one would then have to
ask: How does human language speak of that condition,
whether positive or negative, that awaits us beyond death in
the absence of any clear experience of such a condition? Is this
the reason why the language of eschatology tends to be so rich
in imagery, symbol, and metaphor? Is it just possible, then, that
a metaphorical reading of such language when it appears in
Scripture is in reality the most literal reading?

Whatever we might say about this, it is important in
dealing with any text to distinguish between the medium and
the message. It is certainly possible to be honestly and deeply
concerned about the integrity of the biblical message and still be
convinced that, at many crucial moments, the language of
Scripture is highly symbolic and metaphorical. In fact, this may
be the most appropriate way of expressing that sense of
desperate loss which lies at the core of the idea of hell without
in any way describing such a condition in specifics.

Another factor I find appealing is that the argument
suggests the advisability of studying the broader understanding
of theological language and its own peculiar "logic." It seems
clear that whenever human beings attempt to speak about

ultimate matters—and such is the task of religion and theology—human language begins to do strange things. Hence the significance of religious symbol, analogy, and metaphor. Some awareness of this is an important safeguard against claiming to know "too much." Certainly it is a common temptation among religious believers to seem to know more about the other world (which none has ever experienced) than most of us can claim to know about this world of daily empirical experience. Some sense of the limits of language and the peculiar logic of language about God and ultimate concerns is well advised.

Another appealing aspect of the metaphorical interpretation is that it opens possibilities for exploring the relation between the biblical images of ultimate realities with those of other religious traditions. I have on my desk at this moment a book containing numerous artistic depictions of images contained in the literature of various religious traditions. The book is open to a page that contains a Chinese Buddhist painting. If the faces, garb, and architecture were not so obviously Chinese, the painting could well have been done by a medieval European Christian. While it is not clear what sort of interactions might have been involved between the religions after centuries of missionary work, there seems to be good reason to say that something in the human psyche has produced the same or similar motifs in widely diverse contexts. This needs to be investigated more carefully.

All of these positive aspects of the metaphorical approach point to a more basic and difficult problem. What sort of understanding of revelation are we dealing with? Obviously the treatment of this would move far beyond the scope of Crockett's argument. But at some point, the metaphorical understanding must face this question: Is the text of the Bible identical with the message of divine revelation? Or does the text give witness, in deeply human and limited ways, to a divine communication which never finds appropriate expression in human words and images? It seems to me that the answer to this question is crucial to the larger argument.

Response to William V. Crockett

Clark H. Pinnock

Bill Crockett says that he has not heard a sermon on hell for a long time but gives a different explanation for the silence than Walvoord gives. He does not attribute the reticence of preachers to squeamishness or reluctance to tell the truth but to a mistaken tradition regarding hell's nature. Crockett asks, as I do, how anyone can preach a doctrine that says God condemns people to suffer forever in literal flames. As if God would make sinners like chestnuts roasting on an open fire! When I read Crockett, I feel that I am in the presence of one who understands the problems of the traditional view the way I do, and in ways Walvoord does not.

I agree with him that one cannot preach what the tradition has said about literal hellfire, because it is such a morally and judicially intolerable notion (and one not even necessary according to exegetical considerations). The fact that Augustine and Edwards could have cauterized their consciences into believing it should make no difference at all to us. After all, both men also believed in double predestination as well. One simply has to admit that tradition contains a number of obnoxious things that need changing; so let us be bold to change them. The credibility of the Christian message is at stake—for, as Crockett says, people are not likely to worship a cosmic cook as God.

I also appreciate Crockett's scholarship and his tone of fairness on many issues. For example, he refuses to reject my position of hell as annihilation on the grounds that a group like the Adventists teach the same thing, and he rejects the idea that it is wrong because it is different from what Augustine taught. Many defenders of hell in the tradition stoop to such desperate tactics, and Crockett will have nothing to do with them.

The problem Crockett finds with the tradition about the nature of hell is its literalism. Theologians in the past have misread the true significance of the Bible's eschatological assertions. Hayes and I join with him against Walvoord on this point about misplaced literalism. The matter surfaces in all our chapters. Recognizing that eschatological assertions in the Bible are basically nonliteral in their thrust, Crockett is free to propose a nonliteral view of the nature of hell as his corrective to the tradition. In his view, hell is still understood as everlasting, conscious punishment, but as less literally hellish because physical fire no longer tortures or burns the flesh of the damned. Descriptions of hell, he claims, are not literal but metaphors for something else.

Naturally I agree with Crockett about literalism being part of the problem. Hellfire is a metaphor or analogy for something on another level. There is (I think) a commendable shift here from thinking of punishment extrinsically (like a physical blow) to thinking of it intrinsically (as morally appropriate to the act). Just as the rewards of heaven should not be viewed as cash payments but rather as fulfillment of the love we have for God, so the pains of hell do not extrinsically torture sinners but are an appropriate response to the choices they have made against God.

But we need to know a little more about the reality Crockett thinks hellfire is a metaphor for. Several times he says that he does not know what hell will be like. But how far does this not-knowing extend? Might hell be destruction (as I am contending) or Manhattan at rush hour (like Woody Allen thinks) or a country club? Crockett tells us that hell is a picture of something: I want to know what hell is a picture of. Let me explain why.

Crockett is defending a nonliteral version of hell as everlasting, conscious punishment. We need to know how it may compare to Walvoord's literal version in order to judge whether it is an improvement on it. After all, that's his whole point. Crockett charges the literal position with sadism. I agree, but what if his version of hell turns out to be just as sadistic or more so? What would be gained then? How would shifting to metaphor have helped us?

It seems to me that Crockett leaves us in the dark about the nature of his nonliteral hell. Unlike Jean-Paul Sartre or C. S. Lewis, he offers us no analogies of hell as they understand it. He mentions that Calvin said it would be better to take hellfire metaphorically than literally, but what exactly does "better" mean in this context? I would say that Sartre's nonliteral version of hell is better because, although mentally tough going, there are no flames licking up one's leg. A hell like that, though grim enough and no picnic, would be "better" because it would be less sadistic. Is that what Crockett has in mind? Is he trying to take the hell out of hell? Both Walvoord and I are interested in this question, though for different reasons.

To put the question precisely: Is the nonliteral everlasting, conscious suffering—which the wicked have to endure, according to Crockett—equivalent to or not equivalent to what tradition has said about it? Is the pain of hell of the same intensity or of a less fearful intensity? We have to ask this question because Crockett may be on the horns of a dilemma. If he says that his nonliteral hell is less fearful, then a telling motive surfaces: he wants to take the hell out of hell. I am assuming that mental torment alone would not be as bad as both mental and physical torment. If that is what he is trying to do, both Walvoord and I object to this barefaced attempt to evade plain strong biblical warnings.

But if Crockett means that hell (though nonliteral) is not less fearful, then what has been gained? His position would be burdened by exactly the same problems that burden Walvoord's view. He would still be asking us to believe that God tortures people endlessly and no less severely. The pain quotient would be the same, though the instruments would be mental rather than physical. How is this view any improvement if the effect is the same?

I think I know which it is. Crockett says several things that lead one to conclude that he thinks that the punishment in his nonliteral hell will be the equivalent of or worse than punishment in literal fire. For example, he cites J. I. Packer as saying that the biblical images symbolize realities "far worse" than the literal references would suggest. And Crockett himself adds somewhere else that the fire, though nonliteral, is "a symbol of something far greater." Why then does he come down so hard on Walvoord for being sadistic? Why does he leave the impression that a nonliteral view like his would make it possible to preach about hell again? It seems to me that he has painted himself into the same corner. God is a sadistic torturer.

And I think I know why he has done so. Crockett (and Packer) is looking to his theological right and wants to be seen as orthodox, while making a major shift to a nonliteral view of hell. It is essential in this shift not to appear to the fundamentalists to be making hell easy or nice, because they will jump all over him if that were true. So he must not appear to have lowered the pain quotient in a nonliteral hell (even though I think he has). What he does not seem to notice is the way he has landed himself in much the same quagmire Walvoord is in. According to Crockett's view too, God will still torture people everlastingly, at least as intensively as (maybe more intensively than) the traditional view envisages. Let the reader ask: Has Crockett really solved anything?

Ironically, Crockett may have earned the displeasure of the theological right wing without achieving anything substantial. At least my challenge to the tradition results in a view of the nature of hell that is nonsadistic, whereas his challenge yields nothing particularly helpful. He holds to a metaphorical version of hell as everlasting, conscious punishment, a position that remains so close to the older view that it fails to be a significant improvement on it. It is not any easier to believe or preach. All the old problems remain.

The only way to break with this tradition is to break with it decisively. My view cannot be charged with taking the hell out of hell because the hell of hell is precisely absolute death and termination. As the Bible says, "The wicked will be no more."

Chapter Three

THE PURGATORIAL VIEW

Zachary J. Hayes

THE PURGATORIAL VIEW

Zachary J. Hayes

It is a common task of religion to provide some sense of meaning and direction for human life. Among other things, this generally means that religions deal with the so-called big questions: Where do we come from? Where are we going? How ought we most appropriately take up our life and move to our goal? If this is the common task of religion, Christianity does this in its own distinctive way.

There is a profound sense in which Christianity answers the question of our origin and our goal in one and the same word: God. When all is said and done about our biological and cosmic origins, there is an ultimate sense in which we are not only from our parents, from our family, or from our nation, but finally we are "from God." Likewise, when all speculation about the future of the universe is finished, there is an ultimate sense in which we are simply "for God." St. Augustine formulated this beautifully when he addressed God in the following words: "You have created us for yourself. And our heart is restless until it rests in you."[1]

If our origin is ultimately in God, so is our destiny. And if the question of our ultimate destiny is the heart of what we call "eschatology," there is a sense in which Christian eschatology can be summed up in one word: God. Again, in the words of

---

[1]Augustine, *Confessions*, 1.1.

Augustine, "After this life, God himself is our place."[2] It is in God that we find our ultimate fulfillment. It is in relation to God that we are judged. And it is the final absence of God that is experienced as hellish isolation by the souls of the lost.

Some might see Augustine's view as a radical reduction of Christian eschatology, and it certainly is that. Some Christians may even feel uncomfortable with it, especially if they think that the biblical revelation is a divine communication of detailed information about another world. Clearly such a reduced formulation seems light years away from the elaborate scenario of the last times and the final events that we find in theological books, catechisms, and sermons of Christian churches throughout the ages. From these we get the clear impression that Christian eschatology contains, in fact, a rather detailed geography of the "other world." Some of this information about the "other side" seems related to insights of the Old Testament, and some of it seems similar to literature of other religious traditions. And yet other aspects of this scenario seem to be the fruit of a very active Christian imagination working throughout history.

A common feature of the Christian view of the world beyond is the affirmation of a heaven and a hell. While particular Christian traditions may fill out the details somewhat differently, they do generally agree that there is a final, positive relation with God that we can appropriately call "heaven." And the mainline Christian churches at least agree on the possibility of human life ending in a final disaster which theologians commonly call "hell." In the final analysis, most Christian theologians think of the final condition in these terms. But even here, we need to point out that for some Christians, hell is clearly a fact, while for others it is a possibility, and for yet others, it is a situation that will eventually be overcome.

If the general understanding of Christian eschatology is this two-leveled pattern of heaven and hell, there is a theme in Roman Catholic[3] theology which is not shared by other Christian churches; or at least, if the theme is present elsewhere, it is not understood in the same way. That theme can be

---

[2]Augustine, *Exposition on Psalm 30,* 3.8.

[3]For ecumenical reasons, I shall use the term "Roman Catholic" in deference to those other ancient Christian traditions that view themselves as "catholic" and do not limit the term "catholic" to the Western, Roman tradition.

summarized in the word "purgatory." This word is commonly understood to refer to the state, place, or condition in the next world between heaven and hell, a state of purifying suffering for those who have died and are still in need of such purification. This purifying condition comes to an end for the individual when that person's guilt has been expiated. But as an eschatological "place," purgatory is understood to continue in existence until the last judgment, at which time there will be only heaven and hell. It is this theme of purgatory that concerns me in the present chapter.

PURGATORY AND THE INTERIM PERIOD

I shall begin this exploration of purgatory by distinguishing the concept of purgatory from related issues that might be confused with it. The concept of an interim period, for example, is common in Christian eschatology. It would be easy to confuse the two and to think that purgatory is just another name for the interim state. In fact, this would misunderstand both terms. Though the two concepts are related, they are by no means identical. It is possible to be convinced that there is such a thing as an interim state and to have a specific understanding of what is involved in such a state, and still be totally opposed to the idea of purgatory.

What, then, is meant by the interim period? Simply put, the idea of an interim period is an attempt to answer the question: "What happens to people when they die?" This is not first of all a Christian question. In fact, human beings have reflected on this question throughout history. The Greeks thought of an underworld. It is clear in the Bible that the Jewish vision of death and human destiny has a long and complex history. Ancient Jewish theology simply thought of the "shades" who existed in a condition that was neither good nor bad, but a sort of diminished existence (Gen. 37:35; Ps. 6:5). Only later did the Old Testament come to distinguish reward and punishment in the next life (Dan. 12:1–2). Thus, while the Old Testament had names for various situations beyond this life, Jewish thought is by no means uniform. Yet it provides the context within which Christian reflection on death and the beyond would take place. But the Jewish names for the places in the other world, such as *sheol* and *gehenna*, are not identical with the Christian concept of an interim period.

Christians have their own reasons for thinking of an

interim period. If the term means that a situation exists "in between," it is fair to ask: What is that situation, and what is it "between?" Where does the Christian concept of an interim state come from, and how does it influence the Christian understanding of the afterlife? It is my conviction that the idea of an interim period has its roots in the redemptive work of Christ.

Ever since the proclamation of the resurrection of the Lord, Christians have seen several levels of meaning in the mystery of the resurrection. First, it is a statement about what God has done in Jesus (Acts 2:24). As such, it can be seen as a statement about the personal destiny of Jesus of Nazareth with God. But as humanity is tied to the mystery of the first Adam in the Fall, so it is tied to the mystery of Jesus Christ, the second Adam, in the Resurrection (1 Cor. 15:21–22). This means that the destiny of Jesus as an individual is intrinsically related to the destiny of humanity and the world. Therefore, from the earliest generations of Christian history there has been a sense of completeness together with a sense of incompleteness. What God has done in Jesus is final, decisive, and irrevocable. God has "already" succeeded with eschatological finality in Jesus. But what has happened between Jesus and God has "not yet" worked itself out in the rest of humanity. Here is the basis for the great Christian vision of a "universal human community" in which God's will to save humankind will come to final fruition. In this sense, there is something open-ended and incomplete about the mystery of Christ as long as history continues. It remains incomplete until it has worked itself out in all the redeemed. But that will be only at the end of history (Rom. 8:11, 23–24).

It is this understanding of the mystery of Christ in the early Christian community that led to the conviction that there is something "incomplete" about the situation, not only of believers in history but of those who have died. They are "in between"; that is, between death and that completion which is hoped for with the return of the Lord that brings history to an end. The history of salvation remains incomplete until the end. Therefore, the situation of all individuals remains incomplete until history has run its course.

In the third century, an author such as Origen emphasized this so strongly that he maintained there will be something "incomplete" about the mystery of Christ himself until the whole of his body has been brought to completion. Since, for

Origen and for other early Christian writers, the body of Christ was understood to be the church, the completion of the mystery of Christ (head and body) will arrive only at the end of history when the mission of the church has been completed.

In other words, there is something incomplete about the situation of all who have died before the end of history and the return of the Lord in judgment at the parousia. And this, I believe, is the insight that is expressed in the concept of an interim state when it occurs in Christian theology. This concept says nothing about punishment or reward, but says simply: No individual is fully redeemed until all the redeemed are together in the body (Heb. 11:39–40), united with the head, the one mystery of Christ in its wholeness (cf. Eph. 4:13, 15).

From this it should be clear that Christians can readily think of an interim state without necessarily associating that state with suffering or with purgation. For some it is a state of "sleeping." For Roman Catholic eschatology, it is an active state of being awake. Peculiar to Roman Catholic eschatology is the recognition that the interim state will involve some sort of purgative suffering for those who need it.

The point of our discussion up to here is simply that Christian theology, for Christological reasons, commonly thinks of an interim state. But Roman Catholic theology thinks of this state as a process of purgation or purification for certain needy people. This leads us to the next point: How are we to understand the concept of purification beyond death? This will unavoidably be a discussion of Roman Catholic theology which is not widely shared by other Christian traditions.

PURIFICATION AFTER DEATH

To understand the inner logic of the concept of purification after death, we need to think of a number of interrelated points. First, it is helpful to recall that symbolism about purgation does not begin with Roman Catholicism, nor with Christianity, nor even with the Bible. In fact, such symbolism is widespread in religious history. It is symbolism that reflects a sense of distance between human creatures and God. There is distance, first, because all creatures are limited and finite, while God is infinite. Second, there is distance because human creatures are sinners. Not only are human beings "less than God," they are also "guilty before God." Now, if the concern of the religious journey is to move to ever greater closeness and intimacy with

God in a relationship of love, one must ask how the distance between God and creature might be bridged.

However we might understand the process of bridging this gap (and I will say more about this later), it is common to think of some form of purification in the creature. And that purification is frequently expressed in symbols such as fire. The idea of a purifying fire was present in extrabiblical and in biblical tradition long before the Christian/Catholic concept of purgatory used it in its own way. When such symbolism is used in a Christian context, it expresses the conviction that something happens in the encounter between God and the human creature that makes the creature more "capable" of receiving the gift of divine presence within itself.

A second factor lies in the awareness that most people die with their life projects apparently unfinished, at least as things appear from this side of death. Roman Catholic eschatology sees individual death as the end of a person's individual history, during which time that person's eternal destiny is decided. There is no return to this life for a second chance. Yet most of us do not die as giants of faith. Therefore, it is unlikely that we shall immediately share the destiny of the heroic martyrs of faith. In other words, if we think of heaven as a condition of mutual and unhampered love between God and the human creature, most of us come to the end of our earthly course as flawed lovers, still incapable of love that is deep, broad, and sustained. This seems to be clear enough in the case of our human relations. It seems also to be true of our relation with God. But the final meaning of salvation is not only that God loves us but that we also love God in return. If, from this side of death, we seem to be flawed lovers, and if the condition called heaven involves the perfection of love, how can we possibly bridge that distance?

If we are not quite ready for heaven at the time of death, neither do we seem to be evil ogres. If, theologically, we cannot get the masses of mediocre Christians into heaven, is it really possible that all these millions over the ages wind up in hell with Satan and his minions for all eternity? Clearly St. Augustine felt something of this dilemma. He reflects on his own mother's death in these terms, and he speaks frequently about the cleansing suffering that awaits those who die without being adequately purified in this life.[4] Augustine was much concerned with the moral significance of human life and with the moral continuity between this life and the next. Because of this continuity, he could envision a process of cleansing on both sides of death. He argues that it is better to be cleansed in this life than the next, for the cleansing process in the next life will be far more severe than anything experienced in this life. This was at the heart of his answer to those who felt that purgatory could too easily become an excuse for moral laxity.

Cyprian of Carthage sensed the same dilemma when he was confronted with the problem of basically good people who had failed the test of heroic martyrdom in the time of persecution. Cyprian was clear and unambiguous about the heavenly destiny of heroic martyrs who were victims of the persecution. He was equally clear on the definitive character of hell. His problem had to do with the fate of the well-intended Christians who had weakened under persecution. What was one to think of them? Were such basically good people to be consigned forever to hell? This was a pastoral problem for Cyprian, as it might be for any thoughtful person with deep Christian convictions.[5]

The idea of a process of purification not only in this life but in the next as well seemed to Cyprian a welcome way out of an otherwise uncomfortable dilemma. We could argue that, with Cyprian, the central insight of what eventually became the doctrine of purgatory was formulated already by the middle of the third century. And the impulse of this insight had an interesting effect on other issues. As long as there was only heaven or hell, it was not surprising that hell would be heavily populated. But when the possibility of a purification after death entered the scene, with it came the tendency to depopulate hell by placing many people in a sort of outer court of heaven until they were more fully prepared for entrance into the presence of God.

We can now see how the idea of an interim state for some people could be thought of as a temporary process of purgative suffering. But we are not yet at the full concept of purgatory as known in the Roman Catholic tradition. Another factor in the

---

[4]Augustine, *Confessions*, 9.13; *Enchiridion*, 18.67–69; *Exposition on Psalm 37*, 3; *City of God*, 21.13, 24.

[5]Cyprian, *Letters*, 55.20.

process that led to the concept of purgatory was the conviction that the living might in some way have an influence on the dead. This point involves an understanding of a human solidarity that transcends the limits of death. That is, from a Christian perspective, the human person is not only an individual but a deeply social being as well. And, in Roman Catholic theology, "grace does not destroy, but builds on and perfects nature." Thus if we are social beings by nature and therefore essentially relational, this fact is not left behind in the area of grace. There is a deep sense in which each of us enters into the lives of others, both in terms of love and grace and in terms of hatred and destruction. The traditional formulae of "original sin" and the "communion of saints" express this sense of solidarity both in evil and in grace.

When this sense of human solidarity and interrelatedness is extended to the area of eschatology, it leads us to ponder the possibility that our solidarity with others in both sin and grace is not limited by death. In fact, if the imperative of Christian love is taken with eschatological seriousness, then it amounts to a summons to love even beyond death. Is it not this basic conviction that comes to expression in the ancient Christian practice of praying for the dead, without which such prayer would be little more than meaningless superstition?

With this, we have some of the central concerns that coalesce in the Roman Catholic concept of a purgatory. Purgatory, as Roman Catholic theology envisions it, involves a process of purification after death for those who need it. It is a process in which the concern of the living for the dead, expressed through prayers and charitable works, may have a beneficial effect on the healing of the dead.

Now, it is clearly possible to say all of this without having a particular place in mind. That is, the language of purgation used in Christian tradition seems first to refer to a process rather than to a specific place. This leads us to our final factor, namely, the concept of a "place" in which this purification is accomplished. In his brilliant study of the history of purgatory, Jacques Le Goff argues that it was first in the late twelfth century that the clear reference to purgatory as a place is found in Christian literature.[6] If this argument is correct, it means that

---

[6]Jacque Le Goff, *The Birth of Purgatory*, trans. A. Goldhammer (Chicago: Univ. of Chicago Press, 1984).

even though many intimations of a purifying process may be found in the early centuries of Christian history, the tendency to think of purgatory as a particular place on the eschatological map was a product of the Middle Ages. And even when purgatory was associated with a special place, it is interesting that this place was not necessarily "extra-terrestrial" but could be thought of as somewhere on this planet.

In summary, the notion of a purgatory is intimately related to the conviction that our eternal destiny is irrevocably decided at the moment of our death and that, ultimately, our eternal destiny can be only heaven or hell. But not everyone seems "bad enough" to be consigned to an eternal hell. And most do not seem "good enough" to be candidates for heaven. Therefore, something has to happen "in between." But this cannot mean a coming back to this life and getting another chance since our destiny is decided at the moment of our death. Therefore, some sort of a cleansing process is postulated between death and the entrance into heaven.

A contemporary Roman Catholic theologian, Cardinal Ratzinger, formulates the concept of purgatory in the following way. Purgatory, he writes, means that there is some unresolved guilt in the person who has died. Hence there is a suffering which continues to radiate because of this guilt. In this sense, purgatory means "suffering to the end what one has left behind on earth—in the certainty of being accepted, yet having to bear the burden of the withdrawn presence of the Beloved."[7] This is not unlike the view presented by Dante in his *Divine Comedy*: the souls in purgatory are those of people who were basically animated by the love of God, but whose lives at other levels were marred by blemishes.[8]

Thus the question of purgatory is not simply the notion of an interim state. This has existed in the past and exists at the present time independently of any notion of purgatory. The Roman Catholic view adds to the concept of an interim state the possibility of real purgation after death while in that interim state, and the possibility of being aided by those who still live on earth.

---

[7]Cardinal Ratzinger, *Eschatology*, trans. A. Nichols (Washington, D.C.: Catholic University of America Press, 1988), 189.

[8]Dante Alighieri, *Divine Comedy, Purgatory*, 9.112–14.

PURGATION IN OTHER TRADITIONS

So far I have argued that while there are symbols of purification in religious systems other than Christianity, the specific doctrine concerning a place of purgation as it is known in the West has come to be associated with the Roman Catholic form of Christianity. In the discussion of the "logic" of this concept, I have mentioned the disparity between the creature and God. Other religious systems, of course, feel a similar disparity or distance between human beings and God. They also attempt to bridge that distance in a way similar to the Roman Catholic doctrine of purgatory.

One form of the purifying process in some non-Christian religions is the idea of reincarnation. Because of the distance between where the individual is at the end of life and the final goal of the process of life, the idea of some sort of return to history is used to fill the gap. This return can take place once or many times until the gap has been bridged. While Christians have at times been tempted by the idea of reincarnation, the theory has never become an accepted Christian position. This is probably because it is hard to relate such an idea to the biblical and theological conviction that there is a true finality about death.

Among the forms of reincarnation suggested by Christians, perhaps the most famous comes from the third-century theologian Origen. He argued that at the end of history, the unity of creation would be restored under the rule of God. To him this seemed to be the simple requirement of the goodness of God. In the end, all the enemies of Christ would be overcome, not by being annihilated but by being won over by the divine love. This meant that those who had not made the grade during their first life would return until they had succeeded. Thus the purgative process postulated by Origen is oriented to a theology of universal salvation. In the end, Origen says, there is only "heaven." Even what Christians have called "hell" is seen as a temporary situation that is superseded by a total restoration of all reality to its God-intended form.[9]

Other early Eastern Christian writers envisioned a form of process after death. In the early third century, for example, Clement of Alexandria taught that souls would endure some sort of remedial "fire," a fire that was understood in a

---

[9]H. Crouzel, *Origen* (New York: Harper & Row, 1985), 257ff.

metaphorical sense. The whole vision of Clement was cast in the framework of an understanding of Christian life that saw grace as an increasing God-likeness in the just. Patristic authors commonly used the term "divinization" to express this understanding of grace. It is, of course, the action of God that makes such a process of divinization possible. But Clement envisioned a growing God-likeness, beginning in this life and continuing in the next, until the soul had reached that state of maturity appropriate to its place in the heavenly mansions.[10]

An outstanding expression of the view of the Eastern Fathers is found in Gregory of Nyssa, who writes of the way in which God draws the human person into the divine presence.[11] It is the reality of sin and guilt in the person that makes the divine attraction itself painful. The soul suffers not because God takes pleasure in suffering but because the pain is intrinsic to the encounter between the holy love of God and the still imperfect human being. The intensity of this pain will be proportionate to that evil that remains in the person.

Thus, while the Eastern Christian writers envisioned the possibility of something taking place between death and the full entrance into the presence of God, unlike Western authors, they did not see this as a punitive process of suffering. Rather, they were inclined to think of it as a process of education, maturation, and growth. They therefore used a different set of metaphors than those that became common in the West. Together with this, the Eastern church has maintained a strong sense of the communion of all Christians, whether living or dead, and has valued prayers for the dead. But Eastern theologians have not seen these concerns as sufficient evidence to hold a purgatory as it came to be thought of in the West.

IS PURGATORY SCRIPTURAL?

Whether the doctrine of purgatory can be defended as having any basis in Scripture will depend on how one approaches the Bible and understands revelation. These two issues are closely related to one's understanding of the role of the church in relation to the Bible and revelation. Therefore, it

---

[10]Clement of Alexandria, *Stromata*, 7.10; *Christ The Educator*, 1.61–67.

[11]Gregory of Nyssa, *Oration on the Dead*, in M. J. R. de Journel, *Enchiridion Patristicum* (Freiburg: Herder, 1962), n. 1061.

is necessary to say something about these three issues: revelation, the biblical text, and church tradition.

The history of Christianity indicates that there have always been different ways of approaching the Bible. There has always been great reverence for the text of the Scriptures in Christian communities. But for centuries, beginning with the great Fathers of the Christian tradition, it was felt that the religious meaning of the biblical texts did not lie on the surface. The great events and personalities of biblical history were quite real for the patristic church. But the religious significance of these persons and events and therefore the "revealed message" was sought through a process known as "spiritual interpretation." This process involved a good deal of allegorizing and other techniques of interpretation. This means that texts that were perceived at one level to deal with real historical realities were read at another level in terms of a more symbolic meaning. Thus, while the early Christian writers were convinced that there was a "literal meaning" of the Bible, the real message of revelation was thought to lie at a deeper level of reflection and interpretation. Simply put, the text of Scripture is not in any sense a verbal message from God. The message of revelation is opened to the reader by the operation of the Spirit and not directly by the text of the Bible.

A similar distinction between revelation and biblical text is found today among Christians who accept the basic insights of historical criticism. The texts of Scripture have a long and complex history, and the divine message of revelation is found not in a specific verbal formulation but in a cluster of religious insights that have their own distinctive history. It is from these central insights, derived from the history of the Jewish and Christian people, that Christians come to understand their relation to God and gain insight into his ways of dealing with humanity. The revelation of God is the emergence of this particular form of religious insight. The Scriptures give witness to this revelatory process throughout its historical development. So while the Scriptures remain the privileged and irreplaceable literary point of contact with the basic experiences that lie at the foundation of historic Christianity, there is no specific literary or verbal formula that may simply be identified with the revealed message of God.

From here, the step to tradition becomes clear. In Roman Catholic thought, Christians never deal solely with the text of Scripture. There is also a history of acceptance and interpretation of that text, for no text is self-interpreting. Thus, while there may be profound and divinely inspired insights into God's ways of dealing with humanity at the core of the biblical tradition, the possibility that the Christian community would not grasp the full implications of those insights from the beginning is quite understandable. As the community of faith grew, it reflected on the central events of its history in relation to its ongoing experience. So the possibility of tradition as a growth of understanding and insight into the meaning of the original revelation had to be taken into account.

Now, if the original divine revelation cannot be identified simply with a specific biblical formulation, it should not be surprising to discover that Christian history gives rise to new expressions of faith for which there is no univocal or "literal" warrant in Scripture. The process of testing new formulations in the light of the original revelation and the biblical texts is a necessary and difficult one. But it has long been the conviction of the Roman Catholic church that Christians must reckon with the possibility that not everything was said in the Bible and that new and important insights—and therefore new formulas—may legitimately emerge later in Christian history. This is one aspect of the problem of "tradition." But tradition is not a second source of doctrine next to and independent of the Bible. Rather, it is the living communication of the biblical revelation in ever-changing circumstances and in new and different communities and cultures. Just as the texts of Scripture give witness to the divine revelation, so also does the reality of tradition give witness to the same revelation, but in circumstances unknown to the authors of Scripture.

These ideas must be kept in mind when approaching the doctrine of purgatory. Martin Luther, as we know, claimed that this doctrine had no foundation in the Scriptures. This became a matter of concern for the Council of Trent in its attempt to deal with the issues of the Reformation, and it remains an issue among many Protestant exegetes and theologians today.

Is there a scriptural basis for this doctrine? The Council of Trent maintained that there was, and this conviction has remained in Catholic theology down to the present time. But I must point out that the bishops and theologians at the Council of Trent would have read the Scriptures with the mindset of late medieval people. What warrant they might have seen there for the doctrine would be quite different from that discerned by those contemporary theologians who view the Scriptures through the glass of historical criticism. So we shall discuss the scriptural issue with two perspectives in mind. How would the question have appeared to an earlier generation? And how does it appear today? Is there some basis in the Scriptures for the doctrine of purgatory, or is there not? If we are looking for clear and unambiguous statements of the doctrine, we will look in vain. But our reflections on the matter of tradition and development might suggest a reformulation of the question. We might better ask if anything in Scripture initiated the development that eventually led to the doctrine of purgatory. Or, what is it in the biblical material that generates this form of Christian tradition?

One of the obvious texts in the history of this doctrine is 2 Maccabees 12:41–46, a book which dates back to the second century B.C. In this text some soldiers of Judas Maccabeus had been killed in battle and then were discovered to be wearing pagan amulets. This was a violation of Torah and therefore a serious matter. Judas took up a collection from among his surviving soldiers and sent it to Jerusalem to provide what the text calls an "expiatory sacrifice." This action was motivated by what the author calls a "holy and pious thought." And the final verse of the chapter reads: "Thus he made atonement for the dead that they might be freed from this sin."

For the participants at the Council of Trent in the sixteenth century, this book was part of the biblical canon. It is not surprising that theologians who acknowledged the book's canonical status could see a fairly clear warrant for the idea that good deeds of the living might benefit the dead, and that the dead might be freed of some lesser sins and of some effects of sin even after death. As we have seen, these are basic elements in the doctrine of purgatory. True, the full doctrine of purgatory is not found here, but several crucial elements are. Because of this, Roman Catholic theological handbooks for centuries appealed to 2 Maccabees to show the relation between the church's doctrine and the Scriptures. This all assumes the canonicity of the book. But Maccabees is not included in the Protestant canon, nor is it accepted as a part of the Jewish Bible. Recognizing the problem of canonicity, what might theologians say about such a text at the present time?

Among Roman Catholic exegetes today, the text is seen as evidence for the existence of a tradition of piety which is at least intertestamental and apparently served as the basis for what later became the Christian practice of praying for the dead and performing good works, with the expectation that this might be of some help to the dead. Since the text seems to be more concerned with helping the fallen soldiers to participate in the resurrection of the dead, it is not a direct statement of the later doctrine of purgatory. But like the doctrine of purgatory, it does express some conviction that there are relationships among humans that are not limited by death. This form of piety has strong roots in the long-standing Jewish sense of solidarity, and it is not unreasonable to assume that it later gave rise to the Christian practice of praying for the dead. None of this would have any meaning unless somehow it were possible for God to remit sin in ways not envisioned in our ordinary institutional understandings.

The issue, then, is not whether there is a verbal formulation of the doctrine of purgatory in the Old Testament. It is rather a question of how this sense of piety finds its roots in the Old Testament revelatory process and how, in fact, it develops into a specifically Christian form of understanding concerning the interim condition of the dead. Beyond this, there is no other Old Testament text that stands out clearly in the development of Christian purgatorial doctrine. We turn now to the question of the Christian Scriptures.

In the New Testament, an important text is found in Matthew 12:31–32:

> And so I tell you, every sin and blasphemy will be forgiven men, but the blasphemy against the Spirit will not be forgiven. Anyone who speaks a word against the Son of Man will be forgiven, but anyone who speaks against the Holy Spirit will not be forgiven, either in this age or in the age to come.

One could ask what meaning this text could have if it were not possible that some sins could be forgiven in the next world. This, in fact, seems to be the understanding of Augustine[12] and of Gregory the Great.[13] Likewise, it is the understanding of various medieval popes and councils. This text, therefore, has been seen to provide at least some biblical warrant for the concept of purgatory.

The tendency among exegetes today is to see Matthew 12:31–32 as having little if anything to do with purgatory.

---

[12]Augustine, *City of God*, 21.24.
[13]Gregory the Great, *Dialogues*, 4.39.

Rather, it is understood to refer to the decisive seriousness of one's relation to Jesus who is seen as the Spirit-filled messenger of God. To reject Jesus, who is animated by the Spirit of God, is equivalent to rejecting God. Without indulging us in arcane information about the other world, the text gives an eschatological weight to the rejection of Jesus by saying that such an attitude is a sin that simply cannot be forgiven anywhere at all.

A third important text is 1 Corinthians 3:11–15. Paul is describing the possibility that one person might build a life on the foundation of Jesus Christ while others might build their life on gold, silver, precious stones, wood, hay, or straw. The deeper quality of life may not be apparent in ordinary daily observations, but in the end it will be made known. There will be a "Day" on which the quality of each life will be revealed "with fire." And "fire will test the quality of each man's work." In speaking about the "fire of judgment" the text ends with the remark: "he himself will be saved, but only as one escaping through the flames."

If we take the "Day" to refer to the final judgment, then the text seems to speak of a "fire" after the particular judgment that is involved in individual death. Though it is not necessary to interpret this text to mean the fire of purgatory, it was common among the Latin Fathers to understand this fire as a reference to some sort of transient, purificatory punishment prior to the final salvation. Examples of this interpretation can be found in Augustine[14] and Caesar of Arles.[15] At the present, however, it is common among exegetes to see the "Day" and the "flame" as referring to the final judgment. If that is the case, the text provides no significant basis for the doctrine of purgatory. That is, the "fire" spoken of in this text is not seen as the traditional "fire of purgatory," but rather the "fire of judgment" itself.

In conclusion, we might say that for Christians of earlier generations, it was not difficult to find some basis in Scripture for the doctrine of purgatory, even though each particular text might be subjected to different interpretations. For contemporary readers of the Bible, the actual texts of the Scriptures offer less clear evidence of purgatory than does the history of patristic exegesis. As the time between the resurrection of

---

[14]Augustine, *Exposition on Psalm 37*, 3.
[15]Caesar of Arles, *Sermon 179*.

Christ and the return of Christ at the Last Day became longer and longer, the problem of an interim state between individual death and general resurrection became more acute. But the Scriptures give no clear understanding of how that interim state is to be understood. What does seem clear is that Christians, from the earliest generations, prayed for the dead and believed that such prayer could be of some benefit for them. While these are elements of the later doctrine of purgatory, we are still a long way from the full-blown doctrine as it later came to be known.

Thus Roman Catholic exegetes and theologians at the present time would be inclined to say that although there is no clear textual basis in Scripture for the later doctrine of purgatory, neither is there anything that is clearly contrary to that doctrine. In this they differ from those Protestant theologians who hold not only that the doctrine of purgatory has no scriptural basis but that, in fact, it is contrary to the clear teaching of Scripture. Frequently cited in favor of the Protestant position are: Romans 3:28; Galatians 2:21; Hebrews 9:27–28; and Revelation 22:11. Perhaps Ephesians 2:8–9 says it most clearly: "For it is by grace you have been saved, through faith—and this not from yourselves, it is the gift of God—not by works, so that no one can boast."[16]

A careful reading of these texts reveals that what is at stake here is not the formulations of particular texts of the Bible that unambiguously reject the concept of purgatory. Rather, in each instance, the underlying issue is the Protestant understanding of justification and the classical Protestant problem with a works-theology. The point, then, is not whether Scripture makes the doctrine of purgatory impossible, but whether these passages must lead to the rejection of purgatory when they are interpreted from the perspective of Reformation theology. This latter seems to be the case. But what if the same passages are read from the perspective of a different theology of grace and justification? This, in fact, is what happens when Roman Catholic theologians search the Scriptures for evidence for or against purgatory. Each of these passages can be read in the context of a Roman Catholic theology of grace. What is really at issue, then, is not whether in the light of Scripture purgatory is

---

[16]See Val J. Sauer, *The Eschatology Handbook* (Atlanta: John Knox Press, 1981), 57.

possible or impossible, but whether the Reformation theology of justification provides the only appropriate optical instrument for interpreting the Scriptures.

If Roman Catholic theologians find the evidence of Scripture ambiguous, what follows after that is unavoidably a matter of tradition and the development of church doctrine. And a genuine form of purgatorial understanding was developed rather early in the patristic church. The development came not only from Christian sources, but also from some interaction between Jewish and Christian traditions. The central issue at the core of the development was the sense that some of the dead are in a condition of suffering and can be helped by the prayers of the living. Already at the end of the second century, the *Martyrdom of Perpetua and Felicity* expressed clearly the conviction that Perpetua's prayers for her dead brother had a cleansing and refreshing effect on him.[17] As the specifically Christian development unfolded, it flowed not only from the reading of Scripture but also from the development of the sacrament of the Eucharist and the sacrament of penance in the early church. There is evidence of prayer for the dead already in the second century. And the practice of remembering the dead in the context of the Eucharist existed already in the third century. Eventually, by the third and fourth centuries, there is abundant evidence attesting to celebrating the Eucharist for the benefit of the dead.

HOW THE DOCTRINE OF PURGATORY DEVELOPED

With the problem of development we hit on another area of difference between Roman Catholic and Protestant theology. In its classical formulation, Reformation theology appealed to "Scripture alone." The Roman Catholic understanding embraced in a self-conscious way both the Scriptures and the principle of tradition. For Roman Catholic theology there was not only a sacred text but also a history of acceptance and understanding of the Scriptures. Its classical formulation was the appeal to "both Scripture and tradition."

The issue of Scripture's sufficiency and the Bible's relation to later Christian history has become a self-conscious question

---

[17]*The Acts of the Christian Martyrs*, ed. H. Musurillo (New York: Oxford, 1972), 106–32.

since the time of the Reformation. While the Protestant viewpoint looks for a pure form of doctrine at the beginning of Christian history and sees any deviation from that pure form as a corruption, the Catholic viewpoint sees the beginning more like a seed planted in history. It is the nature of a seed to grow and develop. But the nature of that development as a dimension of the church became the object of considerable theological discussion.

In the course of that discussion, it was never envisioned that the Christian church could be independent of the Bible in its faith life; the Bible was seen as indispensable. Yet it seemed clear to Catholic theology that factors other than the Bible entered into the changing shape of the church over the centuries. Various attempts to explain the difference between the original forms of church life and the present reality of the church have been suggested. The question became particularly important in the nineteenth century. From that time onward, Catholic theologians have been inclined to think of the church as a community that grows through history like a living organism. The idea of a seed and the plant emerging from the seed became common metaphors to express this sense of growth. Like a seed, the revelation of God (and the church formed around that revelation) germinates in the ground of history and of human cultures and gives rise to a plant. While this plant is intrinsically related to the seed, it still looks quite different from the original seed, just as an oak tree looks very different from the acorn from which it grew. In fact, it looks different enough that at any point in history it would be impossible to say that the development would have necessarily had to take this specific form. In terms of doctrine, this has come to mean that, while the Scriptures have a normative and irreplaceable role to play in the faith life of the church, nevertheless, we ought not to expect any one-to-one relationship between the formulations of the Scriptures and the later formulations of church doctrines.

So for Roman Catholic theology, it is not surprising that we cannot find a clear textual "proof" of the doctrine of purgatory in the Scriptures. But we are inclined to ask whether there are issues that lie at the heart of the biblical revelation that find a form of legitimate expression in this doctrine. One way or the other, the issue of purgatory is clearly an issue of development of doctrine.

But what sort of development? One fact is clear: The

doctrine of purgatory was not the invention of theologians. On the contrary, long before theologians became involved, individual Christians prayed for the dead, as I have said above. And in this practice, they were convinced their prayers benefited the dead. In this sense, the question of purgatory can be said to have emerged from the "voice of the people." This insight lies at the core of Le Goff's historical study mentioned earlier, where he concludes that the roots of purgatorial doctrine are found not in some theological theory but in the concrete practice of the faithful. This practice was eventually given official approval by the hierarchy and "purged" of what theologians felt were excessively superstitious elements. As this happened, it became possible to relate the purgatorial belief to the developing Roman understanding of indulgences, a factor that became important during the Reformation. Le Goff's argument offers a helpful way of moving through a very complex history. It also raises some interesting questions about the way in which the reality of faith is carried in the Christian community. In this particular instance, at least, the Christian faithful at large play a decisive role in the process.

Another point of Le Goff's argument revolves around the fact that one can think of a "purgation" without saying anything about a place in which that purgation is to be carried out. Thus there is a movement from a vaguely defined sense of purgation to the specific place where that process occurs. With this, the geography of the "other world" is expanded from the two-level vision of heaven and hell to a three-level vision which includes an intermediate place between heaven and hell. According to Le Goff, Christians had spoken about purgation from the earliest generations of Christian history, but the idea that purgatory was a specific place emerged with clarity only at the end of the twelfth century.

Perhaps the most elaborate expression of the late medieval vision is found in the *Divine Comedy* of Dante. The meaning of "other world" is not necessarily a place outside this created cosmos. To this famous poet, the place of purgation is located on the earth beneath the "starry firmament." It is a mountain in an uninhabited place of the southern hemisphere, directly opposite Jerusalem.[18] In Dante's view, the symbolism of purgation is that of the "climb up the mountain." The point of

---

[18]Dante, *The Divine Comedy*, Purgatory, 2:3 and 4:68ff.

purgation is the "progress" of the soul that becomes purer with each step of its ascent.

If we go back to our original question about the nature of this development, we can summarize Le Goff's view by saying that the development seems to have begun at the level of popular piety and to have moved eventually to official recognition and theological elaboration. Secondly, it seems to have been a movement from symbolism of purgation to the idea of a specific place in which this purgation was carried out. Therefore, for Le Goff the development represents an expansion of the Christian imagination concerning the ultimate relations between God and creation.

CONFRONTATION WITH EASTERN CHRISTIANITY AND WITH THE PROTESTANT REFORMATION IN THE WEST

Even though details of Le Goff's argument may be challenged, the fact remains that the clearest official expressions of the Roman understanding of purgatory are found in a confrontation of the Roman authorities with the Eastern church in the medieval period and with the Reformers of the West in the sixteenth century. In both cases there is little doubt that issues of ecclesiastical power and politics played a significant role in the proceedings. It was out of this context that the official Catholic teaching emerged. By official teaching, I refer to positions taken in the most solemn manner by the Roman Catholic hierarchical teaching office. The official teaching, therefore, is distinct from the speculations of systematic theologians, and in this case is much more limited than the popular understandings of purgatory suggest. The official teaching on purgatory is found in statements made by solemn assemblies of bishops and theologians recognized at least by Roman Catholics as ecumenical councils. In response to the Eastern church, the Second Council of Lyons (1274) and the Council of Florence (1439) addressed the issue. The Council of Trent (1563) did the same in response to the Protestant Reformation.

The point of difference between Rome and the Eastern church is not the same as that between Rome and the Protestant Reformers of the West. The Eastern church, in the aftermath of the Origenist controversy and the rejection of

Origen's theory of universal restoration, held to a view summarized well by John Chrysostom.[19] According to this view, there was indeed an intermediate state for everyone between death and general resurrection. All were situated at various levels of happiness or unhappiness, each in relation to the level of sanctification achieved on earth. The "communion of saints" meant that the saints in happiness could be of help to the faithful still on earth, and the faithful on earth could— through prayer and good works—bring some aid to the souls situated at some level of unhappiness. But the unhappiness was not understood to include atonement or purifying fire. We might envision it more in terms of a process of maturation than as some sort of judicial or penal process. Thus, while the Greeks rejected the idea of punishment or atonement after death, they did not reject the idea that the living could come to the aid of the dead by prayers, works, and above all, by offering the Eucharist for their benefit.

For the sixteenth-century Reformers in the West, however, the issue was quite different. Such pious practices—shared by the East and the West until this time—were seen by Protestant Reformers as a failure to take seriously the sufficiency of Christ's redemptive work. Hence the Reformers objected strenuously to the practice of offering Mass for the benefit of the dead and to the Roman practice concerning indulgences. While the issue of money was involved in both cases, the problem was not simply that. Far more basic was the issue of works in the context of justification and grace. The problem of the Reformation did not begin with the rejection of the Roman Catholic theology of purgatory. But in a sense, the issue of purgatory emerged as the point around which other more basic problems coalesced. These were problems about the relation of the purgatorial doctrine to the Scriptures, the role of the Pope in the remission of sin, and, above all, the sovereign freedom of God in all things pertaining to grace and justification. Luther and other Reformers seemed to think that the doctrine of purgatory would obscure the grace and redemptive work of Jesus.

---

[19]See J. Pelikan, *The Spirit of Eastern Christendom* (Chicago: Univ. of Chicago Press, 1974), 279–80, 293; also J. N. Karmiris, "Abriss der dogmatischen Lehre der orthodoxen katholischen Kirche," in P. Bratsiotis, *Die orthodoxe Kirche in griechischer Sicht*, 2d ed. (Stuttgart, 1970), 15–120, esp. 113–17.

The conciliar teaching on purgatory is very concise. The Council of Lyons stated that those who die in charity and are truly sorry for their sins, but before they have made complete satisfaction for their wrongdoings, will be purged after death by "cathartic punishments." The council showed considerable restraint by avoiding any reference to purgatory as a particular place, even though the idea had existed for about a century by this time. The Council of Florence added nothing substantial to the teaching of Lyons. This council is interesting more for the discussions of ecclesiological problems and issues of method than for any advance in the theology of purgatory.

The teaching of the Council of Trent, like that of Lyons, is brief. Trent reduces its teaching on purgatory to two points. First, purgation exists for some between death and the general resurrection, and second, the souls undergoing such purgation can be aided by the prayers and good works of the faithful and especially by the sacrifice of the Mass. Beyond this, nothing is said about the location of purgatory or the nature of the "fire." The Council does not even say clearly that purgatory is a place, though its teaching is commonly understood to mean that. And the Council takes the occasion to encourage the bishops to eliminate all superstitious understandings and practices from their communities. Church leaders should take measures to avoid "things that pander to a certain kind of curiosity and superstition or savor of filthy lucre."

To this extent, the Council of Trent recognized what it saw as the legitimate concern of the Reformers and tried to initiate action against the aberrations which the Reformers decried. But it never conceded the fundamental soteriological doctrine of the Reformers. Insofar as this involves a different understanding of the relation between God and humanity, between grace and freedom, and between faith and works, the issue remains for ecumenical relations even today. The most basic issue in the entire discussion, in my view, is not the existence or non-existence of purgatory, for that question is symptomatic of a much deeper issue. At root, the ecumenical problem is a question of different soteriological perceptions. To this I now turn my attention.

PURGATION AND THE UNDERSTANDING
OF GRACE AND JUSTIFICATION

As we have seen, the concept of purgatory does not stand alone as a theological idea. Rather, it is part of a larger scenario that reflects the Roman Catholic understanding of how God deals with us and how we are to respond to God in the context of grace and eschatological fulfillment. The problem with purgatory might be seen as an eschatological extension of the Roman Catholic understanding of grace and works. How do human works play into the theology of grace? Do works in any way put God under obligation to us? In what sense can we speak of the freedom of God with respect to grace and how does this relate to our sense of human freedom and responsibility? If there is a problem concerning works already in the understanding of this life, it is not surprising to see the same problem in the eschatological concept of purgatory. I shall now offer some reflections on what this looks like from a Roman Catholic perspective, for in the final analysis, this issue lies at the center of the historical rejection of purgatory from Reformation theology.

One of the crucial convictions of Christianity, whether in its Protestant or Roman Catholic form, is the mystery of God's limitless love, forgiveness, and acceptance. For Christian theology, it is the creative power of God's love that brought forth the created universe, conferring on it the very gift of existence. It is the same mystery of God's creative love that brings the potential of created being to fulfillment in eschatological completion. And it is that forgiving, merciful love that reaches to us through the historical mediation of Jesus Christ. For Roman Catholic theology, this has long meant that the language of grace does not begin with the doctrine of redemption. It begins already, at least in an analogous way, with the doctrine of creation. For existence itself is a free and unmerited gift from the creative love of God. Salvation, then, is the realization of the full potential of human existence in that sort of relation to God which is possible for us only because God makes our freedom possible and crowns the act of our freedom with the transforming power of the divine presence in human life. In such a context, Christ is seen to be the supreme realization of that potential to receive God into human life and hence to find final fulfillment. It is to this mystery of Christ that Christians look to discover the deepest meaning of grace and salvation.

Roman Catholic theology understands our created existence to be but the beginning of a process that comes to complete fruition through a life of response to the continuing offer of God's gracious presence in human life. We are, so to say, enveloped by grace. Grace is the first word (creation), and grace is the final word (the fulfillment of creation with God). Grace is with us always, calling us out of a fallen, self-centered existence to an existence in love, sustaining us in our halting efforts to respond generously to God, and crowning our efforts with the rich gift of God's self-communication. Truly, God is the first and the final word.

For Roman Catholic theology, God's gracious action is first of all an offer. As such, it is intended to initiate a dialogue with God's free creatures. But that offer does not "come home" unless it is received and responded to by the human person. Grace makes our human response possible. But grace does not do what only we can do, namely, offer an appropriate human response to the mystery of God's love. As Augustine writes: "His mercy comes before us in everything. But to assent to or dissent from the call of God is a matter for one's own will."[20] And in one of his sermons Augustine says: "He who created you without your help does not justify you without your help."[21]

Thus Roman Catholic theology recognizes the possibility that God's offer of grace might be rejected and that the offer might be truly "inefficacious." The doctrine of justification in its Roman Catholic form, then, does not involve a denial of God's gracious initiative, nor of Christ's crucial, mediatorial role in salvation. Neither does the doctrine of purgatory. But both of these doctrines involve a fundamental recognition of the moral significance of human choices in working out the divine plan of salvation. Both these doctrines express the conviction that without a human response, God's initiative remains inefficacious and that God never overrides or suppresses human freedom.

Now, our response to God's grace during our life on earth may be basically good, but it is far from perfect. Here we touch on another difference between Roman Catholic and Protestant theology. This difference provides a helpful basis for seeing that there is a genuine form of "both just and sinner" in the Roman Catholic understanding of justification and grace. For Roman Catholic theology, however, this polarity of grace and sin is internal to the human person. Roman Catholic theology

[20]Augustine, *On the Spirit and the Letter*, 34, 60.
[21]Augustine, *Sermon 169*, 11.13.

thinks of grace as involving a real transformation of the human person in and through its response to God's presence. This is the issue involved in the Roman Catholic tendency to talk about "created grace" and about an increase of grace. The impact of God's gracious presence does not remain "outside" the human person, but touches the very roots of our personal existence. We become different than we were—but not instantly. We become different through a process of transformation spread over a lifetime. The Roman Catholic theology of justification and grace has stronger ties with the Eastern patristic understanding of "divinization" than with the Reformation understanding of "forensic justification."

For Roman Catholic theology, then, the issue of works-theology is not a question of placing God under obligation to us, nor is it a question of producing grace by means of human works. What is really involved here is the conviction that the gift of God to the human creature really changes the creature internally to the degree that the creature is open and responsive to that gift. The issue of "merit" from good works, then, does not mean that we receive something extrinsic to the work itself. We receive nothing other than the very self-gift of God. And in the reception of that gift, we are profoundly changed. What we "get," then, is the intrinsic effect of God's presence on the human person. If we were to think of the relationship between God and the human person as analogous to a relationship of love between two persons, we could say simply that we are changed profoundly in the power of God's presence. And there are two dimensions to this change: the first is the experience of love itself. In a very deep sense, love is its own "reward." The second dimension is that one who has been loved and has loved in return becomes capable of loving more deeply. This is the heart of the matter that Roman Catholic theology commonly expresses in the metaphorical language of "merit." Unfortunately, that metaphor is frequently understood as a reward extrinsic to the very relation of love which grace involves. Language about works and merit, then, begins to sound like an otherworldly bank transaction and becomes problematic not only for Protestant thought but for Roman Catholic thought as well.

We might summarize the Roman Catholic view by saying that human freedom and human response to God must have a place in the final understanding of justification and grace. Unless we attempt to name that place appropriately, the affirmation of grace would turn human beings into automatons. We have not said enough about justification if we speak only of the power of God's gracious action on our behalf. While grace and justification are the free and unmerited offer of God (and in this sense are "from God alone"), yet God's offer is not successful unless it calls forth an appropriate human response. While grace makes the free human response possible, God does not force or take away human freedom and responsibility. The Roman Catholic understanding of grace and freedom sounds more like a dialogue—certainly not a dialogue between equals, but a true dialogue nonetheless—while the Protestant understanding, at least to Roman Catholic ears, sounds like a divine monologue. The Protestant problem with purgatory, it seems to me, does not begin in the afterlife. It begins already in this life, in the doctrine of justification and grace.

CONCLUSION

I have tried to provide some insight into the broader eschatological context for the concept of purgatory, a sense of the inner logic of this theological position, and at least some awareness of the sources from which this doctrine evolved. It remains to indicate where it stands on the theological map of contemporary Roman Catholicism.

As Le Goff has argued, the historical development of purgatory was, at least in part, a movement from symbolism about purgation to the imaginative creation of a place in which this purgation would take place. Contemporary Roman Catholic experience seems to be well along the way in the reversal of that process. While many Roman Catholics reflect very little change in their understanding of purgatory and of the practices associated with it, recent decades show a remarkably large vacuum in the case of many other Roman Catholics. The official teaching of the Roman Catholic Church has not changed on the major points affirmed by the councils mentioned above, but the practice of many Roman Catholics and the reflection of many theologians have shifted significantly.

Not knowing what to do with this "place" in the other world, contemporary theologians tend to situate a process of purification within the experience of death itself. Death is, in much of contemporary Roman Catholic thought, the moment of our final decision for or against God. And that which "purges" us is not some external thing, but the very mystery of the holy

God. If we are flawed lovers during life, how will we respond to God's summons in the ambiguous darkness of death? Will our death be a hardening in sin leading to hell? Or will it be a final opening to the mystery of God's love coming to us from beyond death? Or will the layers of selfishness we have built up in this life make it painful for us to "let go" and finally to entrust ourselves to the embrace of God's love and mercy in the darkness of death?

Purgatorial theology envisions the latter as a real possibility. This modern tendency among Roman Catholic theologians has a stronger affinity with the theology of the Eastern church than with the medieval extravagances of the West, but it is clarified now through contemporary explorations into the experience of human death. In this context, purgation is seen as a symbol of the full maturation of a person's decisive choice for God and of the full integration of that choice into all the dimensions of that person's being.

This might seem to heighten the significance of individual eschatology excessively. But it is commonly placed in a context that recognizes how deeply each individual life is embedded in a network of relationships. While our personal history is decisively finished at death, each of us leaves behind a network of failures and painful experiences that enter into the lives of others.

Is it possible to see this as an intimation in our contemporary experience of what was traditionally pointed to with the symbol of the communion of saints? Our personal lives are decisively ended with death, but we may not yet have integrated the fundamental option of our lives into all the dimensions of our own personal being. Much less have we succeeded in healing the impact that our lives have had on others. According to a thought-provoking essay by Robert Schreiter, the core issue that lies behind the tradition might be seen as the basic human need to deal with the consequences of our lives, both for ourselves and for others.[22] For those who are convinced that there is an abiding issue behind the history of this doctrine, this is a title that aptly describes the present situation in Roman Catholic thought.

---

[22]Robert Schreiter, "Purgatory: In Quest of an Image," *Chicago Studies* 24 (1985), 2.167ff.

Response to Zachary J. Hayes

John F. Walvoord

The exposition and defense of the purgatorial view of hell are most revealing. Although delineating the Roman Catholic view of hell, and specifically purgatory, with skill, the treatment itself provides all the necessary ingredients for rejecting the doctrine of purgatory.

Purgatory Is Based upon the Allegorical School of Interpretation at Alexandria. Hayes quotes with approbation the church father Origen, whom some biblical scholars, both Protestant and Roman Catholic, view as heretical. Origen and other church fathers like him maintained that the entire Bible should be interpreted allegorically; such a hermeneutical method defeats not only eschatology but all other major areas of theology as well. Hayes practically admits this when he states: "The purgative process postulated by Origen is oriented to a theology of universal salvation."

Purgatory Depends Upon Apocryphal Writings. As the discussion makes clear, the major passage in support of purgatory is found in 2 Maccabees 12:41–46, an apocryphal writing accepted by the Roman Catholic Church but not by Protestant theologians. This is their major proof text and is a tacit admission that the Bible itself does not have a clear teaching on this subject.

The Doctrine of Purgatory Depends upon "Revelation" Given to the Roman Church in the Middle Ages. In appealing to the authority of the church, especially as it existed in the Middle Ages, Hayes's treatment obviously departs from a credible basis for belief among many Protestants. Not only does it teach post-biblical revelation but, in a sense, claims that such additional revelation was given in harmony with Roman Catholic doctrine; this is not the Protestant point of view. Again, this is a tacit confession that the Bible itself does not teach purgatory.

Biblical References Do Not Teach the Doctrine of Purgatory. Hayes's presentation states, "Thus Catholic exegetes and theologians at the present time would be inclined to say that although there is no clear textual basis in Scripture for the later doctrine of purgatory, neither is there anything that is clearly contrary to that doctrine." This, of course, Protestant theologians would deny, because the doctrine of punishment is declared to be "for ever and ever" (Rev. 20:10).

References to 1 Corinthians 3:11–15 have no indication that the judgment is remedial; the bad works declared to be burned up relate to rewards, not to one's eternal salvation. The use of the statement that blasphemy of the Spirit cannot be forgiven (Matt. 12:30) does not give grounds for belief that it can be forgiven in the next world. Matthew 12:32 plainly states, "Anyone who speaks against the Holy Spirit will not be forgiven, either in this age or in the age to come." This is hardly a ground for a purgatorial judgment that provides retribution.

The Doctrine of Purgatory Requires an Inaccurate Definition of Grace. There is obviously a fundamental difference in the Roman Catholic and Protestant views of salvation. This is recognized in Hayes's chapter when he states that the Council of Trent "did not concede the fundamental soteriological doctrine of the Reformers." The chapter speaks of "the mystery of God's limitless love, forgiveness, and acceptance." The problem is that God's love, while it is infinite, is limited in its application to those who receive Christ as Savior, and the same applies to grace, forgiveness, and acceptance. Even a merciful and gracious God cannot forgive one who has rejected Christ. It is true that grace is not a merited gift based upon works, but it is also true that grace extends to all sins as contained in the simple idea that when Christ died, he died for all the sins of the world, not just some. To some extent, the chapter recognizes this. The question is whether grace is sufficient to save a Christian "who is far from perfect," as the chapter mentions. Obviously, if perfection is required, nobody is saved. But does retribution in hell provide that perfection?

The Position of the Contemporary Roman Catholic Church on Purgatory Keeps Changing. Hayes himself admits that "the official teaching of the Roman Catholic Church has not changed on the major points affirmed by the councils mentioned above, but the practice of many Roman Catholics and the reflection of many theologians have shifted significantly." This change is somewhat defined in his statement that "contemporary theologians tend to situate a process of purification within the experience of death itself," hence making a long purgatorial experience unnecessary.

In brief, if the Protestant view of the Bible and its interpretation is accepted, even if there be some allowance for nonliteral interpretation, it still falls far short of supporting the Catholic doctrine of purgatory. For the most part, the treatment as presented supporting the doctrine of purgatory is its own refutation.

Response to Zachary J. Hayes

William V. Crockett

It is impossible to read Zachary Hayes's chapter on purgatory without being struck by the fair and balanced tone of it all. He discusses the interim state of the dead, but makes no attempt to hide any of the difficulties inherent in the Roman Catholic approach. His comments can, in fact, be wholly disarming. When he cites the purgatory proof text, 2 Maccabees 12:41–46, he cautions that sixteenth-century Catholicism accepted Maccabees as part of the canon, unlike Jews and Protestants, who never recognized it as part of the Bible. In the same vein, when he provides the two New Testament texts that have in times past been used to support the doctrine of purgatory (Matt. 12:31–32; 1 Cor. 3:11–15), he grants that present-day Catholic readers of Scripture may not find the evidence of purgatory as convincing as earlier generations.

Such frank admissions prepare the reader for Hayes's real argument, that Protestant justification by faith might not be the best way to interpret Scripture. Perhaps Scripture (and the doctrine of purgatory) should be seen more broadly—through the lens of a Roman Catholic theology of grace. Protestants, says Hayes, continually look for pure doctrine at the beginning of Christian history (in the New Testament), and any deviation from that pure form is considered corruption. But Roman Catholics see the beginning more like a seed that grows and develops. Thus, the lack of clear biblical texts to support the doctrine of purgatory is secondary. What is important is how God deals with his creation in the context of grace. God is a loving, forgiving God who is full of grace and acceptance. He creates us for himself and sends forth his Son; and in his very act of creation, he extends an offer. What is this offer? Dialogue, says Hayes. God wants a dialogue with us. We as created beings are invited to dialogue with God, to respond to his love. But too often our response to God's grace is wholly inadequate. We do not participate in the dialogue as we should.

And this is the problem, says Hayes. Most of us during our earthly sojourns do not respond fully to God's gracious offer. We come to the ends of our lives, not as giants of faith, but as flawed people incapable of the kind of love God demands. We are not ready for heaven, with its mutual and unhampered love between God and creature, but neither are we evil enough for the darkness of hell. Clearly, some form of purgation must ready us for the light of heavenly relationships, says Hayes, whether it be in the last moments of death or in some "place" where purgation can melt the layers of resistance we have built up.

Protestants have always found the traditional doctrine of purgatory, an intermediate "place" between heaven and hell, inadequate because of the lack of biblical support. Hayes acknowledges this and talks about purgatory as a process that begins at death and continues for those who need it. Where or how it takes place is not important. Neither is the lack of explicit texts a concern because the concept of purgative theology is more like a seed than a planted tree.

Hayes distances himself from the historic Roman Catholic position that sees purgatory as an actual place of cleansing, a kind of medieval horror chamber where sinful believers are readied for the presence of God. Instead, he prefers the recent trend in Catholicism which views death as the moment of final decision for or against God. In the ambiguous darkness of death, he says, God summons us to himself, and how we respond to God's love and mercy will determine our ultimate destinies.

Hayes never discusses whether this purgative cleansing is instantaneous or takes place over a period of time. I suspect he thinks it depends on the layers of selfishness and depravity each person has built up. So although Hayes's purgatory differs somewhat from the traditional Roman Catholic view, it shares the essential idea that most believers are not ready for the presence of God and need a period of cleansing.

Protestants, of course, find it odd that no biblical texts

support purgatorial doctrine. Even if we grant Hayes's seed theology hypothesis, we should at least find some good hardy apostolic seeds from which the doctrine is built. Hayes tries to solve this problem by appealing to the concept of solidarity. Just as individuals participate in the sin of Adam, he says, so also do they participate in the communion of saints. This means that the prayers and charitable works of believers may improve the situation of the dead. This should not surprise us, he argues, because the solidarity of humanity has always affected the individual. The history of salvation has yet to work itself out, and until the return of the Lord, the situation of all individuals remains incomplete.

With this last statement, Hayes's position becomes clearer. He thinks that death is a step—but not the final step—in the soul's ascent to God. As death claims souls, God comes to them and gives them another opportunity to respond to his grace. This opportunity is the extended period we commonly call purgatory. No matter how they respond, their situations remain, for better or worse, incomplete until the coming of the Lord. Prayers and charitable deeds done in their behalf, therefore, can improve their post-mortem conditions and hasten the transition from purgatory to heaven.

If I have not distorted the picture Hayes is presenting, I wonder how it fits with the apostolic tradition reflected in the New Testament. When Paul talks about solidarity with Adam (Rom. 5:12–21; 1 Cor. 15:20–28), he means, as Hayes correctly points out, that all humanity in some sense participates in Adam's sin. When Adam and Eve disobeyed God, they opened the floodgates of sin so that forever after their offspring would be infected by the disease of sin. When the apostle talks about solidarity with Christ in the same texts, he means that all who put their faith in Christ, the second Adam, are freed from the dominion of sin and death. Sin's hold is broken by the power of the resurrection, and believers are in Christ. What does this teaching have to do with purgatory?

For Hayes it shows solidarity. He thinks there is a parallel between the influence of sin on humanity and the influence of kindly deeds on the departed. But Paul is saying nothing of the sort. He wants to show that there are two realities, two solidarities: those who are in Adam, and those who are in Christ. Those in Adam go the way of death (1 Cor. 15:22); they are "unbelievers" (1 Cor. 6:6), who "belong to the night" (1 Thess. 5:4–11) and do not know God (Gal. 4:8). Those in

Christ go the way of life (1 Cor. 15:22); they are "saints" (Rom. 1:7), who are "sons of the light" (1 Thess. 5:4–11) and who are "known by God" (Gal. 4:9).

The concept of solidarity in Paul's letters may perhaps be extended to include the idea of believers in the community helping each other and praying for one another, but this has nothing to do with purgatory or with the prayers of saints influencing the fate of the dead. If we were to follow Hayes's "solidarity" theology to its conclusion, we would have saints in heaven praying or doing good deeds for the benefit of the living (and perhaps he holds that view, I don't know).

The real reason for purgatorial theology comes about because most believers do not seem ready to meet God. Paul, in effect, acknowledges this concern when he says that we who die in Christ need not fear the judgment because Christ "is at the right hand of God . . . interceding for us" (Rom. 8:34). With Christ as our advocate, our lawyer, the natural fear of inadequacy falls aside. We are "in Christ" and therefore suffer "no condemnation" (Rom. 8:1). We have no fear of being separated "from the love of God that is in Christ Jesus" (Rom. 8:35–39). Death is "swallowed up in victory" (1 Cor. 15:54), and we rejoice that even if our earthly bodies are destroyed, we have a heavenly body prepared by God (2 Cor. 5:1–5). When the Lord comes in his glory, he will gather his people to himself, and we shall forever be with him in heaven (1 Thess. 4:13–18).

The point is that in solidarity with Christ, believers *already* have forgiveness of sins (Rom. 8:31–39; Col. 1:14). As Paul said: "If righteousness could be gained through the law [through our good deeds], Christ died for nothing" (Gal. 2:21). To suggest, as Hayes does, that most believers are not ready for heaven, smacks of the kind of works theology Paul so strongly opposed. Such grace might not seem deserved, but it nevertheless is the possession of those justified in Christ (Rom. 5). When Christ returns, the saints do not have to be readied for heaven, but will "meet the Lord in the air" and will be "with the Lord forever" (1 Thess. 4:17–18). Their citizenship is "in heaven," and at the coming of the Lord, God will transform their "lowly bodies so that they will be like [Christ's] glorious body" (Phil. 3:20–21). Believers have confidence because they know that being "away from the body" means being "at home with the Lord" (2 Cor. 5:8), even as the apostle expressed the same confidence for himself, were he to die (Phil. 1:21–23).

The concept of purgatory constructed by Hayes is reasonable in light of the shortcomings all of us share. There is no doubt that in ourselves we are ill-prepared for the glory of heaven. But by God's grace we are *in Christ*, and it is on this basis that we enter God's presence.

How reasonable, then, is the doctrine of purgatory? If we have no evidence that Jesus or the apostles ever taught the doctrine—even in a weak seed form—and if indeed they assumed that death or the Second Advent ushered believers immediately into the presence of God, where does that leave purgatory? It leaves it, I should think, as a later invention of the church.

Response to Zachary J. Hayes

Clark H. Pinnock

The problem in responding to Zachary Hayes is not the quality of his work (which is excellent) but its focus and orientation. He writes little about hell and much about purgatory, in contrast to the other chapters that concentrate only on hell. Hayes has opened up a new subject—the issue of purgatory, a topic natural to him as a Catholic writer but foreign to Protestants. His chapter changes the direction of the book. Nevertheless, it gives me permission to explore an interesting issue: Is there room in evangelical theology for a doctrine of purgatory and, if so, what kind of purgatory?

Hayes has written a whole book on eschatology, entitled *Visions of the Future, A Study of Christian Eschatology* (Wilmington, Del.: Michael Glazier, 1989). This gives me additional insight into his views of hell, though little is said about it in the chapter. I find Father Hayes to be a learned, fair, and orthodox theologian. I encounter in his chapter reasoning which is subtle, balanced, and sound, coupled with careful scriptural exegesis. He typifies the kind of Catholic scholar from whom we evangelicals can learn. We share with such theologians respect for the Scriptures and church traditions and a desire to integrate what we learn with the best modern insights. Our own theological performance can only be improved from dialoguing with colleagues such as Hayes.

First, I would assure the reader that Hayes believes in both hell and purgatory, as the Catholic tradition does, and is not suggesting here that hell is purgatory or that it leads all souls to heaven. For Hayes, as well as the rest of us in the book, hell is the final destiny of impenitent sinners, from which there will be no exit. I am glad that he is not a universalist, for scriptural warnings about destruction would seem to rule that out.

Hayes also tells us why hell exists, and his explanation appeals to the Arminian streak in me. Hell, he maintains, is a necessary implication of human freedom. Just as heaven is possible if we accept the grace of God, so hell is possible if we refuse it. God has given human beings the power to make fundamental choices that have eternal consequences. They can choose salvation or damnation. God does not save people against their will, and the existence of hell underlines how seriously he takes the gift of freedom. Universalism is not a viable position because of the gift of human freedom. (This point has been made with particular force in the last century by Nicolai Berdyaev and in this century by Karl Rahner.)

To be a universalist one really has to have to work with a predestinarian theology. How would it even be possible for God to save everyone if not by forcing some to be saved who do not want that? Some would have to be saved against their will. Now, if one is a predestinarian and a denier of human freedom, universalism is possible. In such theologies, God is always forcing people to do what they do not want to do. All that would have to happen for universal salvation to result would be for God to increase the number of elect to one hundred percent and save everybody by sovereign (coercive) grace. Nor is this just possible—if God is gracious and has this kind of coercive power, one must suppose God would do exactly this in his mercy. One might posit that a Christian who is predestinarian ought to be a universalist in principle. A good God who could save everyone surely would save everyone. But Hayes and I are not universalists because we are not predestinarians.

It is not clear what Hayes thinks about the nature of hell, though. I know that he believes in the fact of hell, but I cannot tell what he thinks about its nature. From comments on biblical hermeneutics, I can deduce that he supports a metaphorical rather than a literal view of hell; that is, he stands with Crockett, not with Walvoord. But I am not sure whether he would opt for everlasting conscious torment or the annihilationist view—that is, whether he stands with Crockett or with me. This is not clear either in his book or in this chapter.

Assuming the role of a detective, I note that the official Catholic view is one of the nature of hell as everlasting conscious punishing, so I could conclude Hayes probably agrees with Crockett, not with me. One statement early in his chapter suggests as much: "It [hell] is the final absence of God that is experienced as hellish isolation by the souls of the lost." This suggests to me that sinners have an unending experience of separation. Also, the fact that Hayes draws on Karl Rahner, and knowing that this is Rahner's position, leads me to the same conclusion. (On Rahner's eschatology, see Marie Murphy, *New Images of the Last Things* [Ramsey, NJ.: Paulist Press, 1988]). On the other hand, there is a possibility that Hayes's professed agnosticism about the nature of hell might extend to that very distinction. If we do not know the nature of hell, then any position might turn out to be true, mine just as well as Crockett's. (Since Crockett says he does not know what hell will be like, the same applies to him.)

Finally, let me comment on his views about purgatory and consider whether there could be an evangelical version of this doctrine. Belief in purgatory is an ancient tradition just as everlasting conscious punishment is, so I do not see how it can be ruled out of consideration by evangelicals. Perhaps it has even more credibility as a tradition. Ironically, I rather think that it actually does.

Although not accustomed to thinking much about purgatory because I have shared the knee-jerk rejection against it in evangelical thinking, I have to admit that Hayes makes good sense in his defense of it. I cannot deny that most believers end their earthly lives imperfectly sanctified and far from complete. I cannot deny the wisdom in possibly giving them an opportunity to close that gap and grow to maturity after death. After all, most evangelicals accept the position that babies dying in infancy end up in heaven. If so, do they live in heaven as babies or as grown persons? If we think they will be grown persons, where do we suppose that they grow to maturity?

Obviously, evangelicals have not thought this question out. It seems to me that we already have the possibility of a doctrine of purgatory. Why would there not be provision made for growth and development between death and entry into heaven? Surely it would be a good thing if the decision for God on earth were integrated into all dimensions of life. Ask yourself, are you not going to need some finishing touches in the area of holiness when you die? Why should we stick to the assumption that growth can take place only on earth before death?

I admit it; Hayes got me to thinking about this as an area of evangelical doctrine which may need opening up. I am not, of course, the first one to think of it. There are many respected theologians who have thought the same. One finds sympathy with an idea of purgatory in George MacDonald, J. B. Phillips, William Barclay, and many others. C. S. Lewis believed in purgatory. In *Letters to Malcolm: Chiefly on Prayer* (San Diego: Harcourt, Brace, Jovanovich, 1973, pp. 108–9), he says, "Our souls demand purgatory, don't they?" He was reasoning in the following way: When we arrive at heaven's door still polluted and dirty, would we not want to be cleaned up before entering in, even if it were a painful experience? Of course we would, Lewis says. Well, that is what purgatory does. It makes us fit for service above.

I would defend a doctrine of purgatory in this way. It is obvious that Christian character is not perfectly transformed at death. Therefore, it is reasonable to hope that there might be a perfecting process after death. Without discounting the decisiveness of decisions made in this earthly life, a doctrine of purgatory would allow for continued growth in the same direction. The patriarch Job believed in God and lived by faith even though he knew little about God and would have died imperfectly sanctified. Somehow Job must be made ready for the life of heaven with the triune God. Evangelicals would not think of purgatory as a place of punishment or atonement because of our view of the work of Christ, but we can think of it as an opportunity for maturation and growth. God's plan is to make us holy and, if this is not achieved at death, I would assume that it will be completed afterwards, until the work is finished. I find it satisfying to think that death does not stop the process of growth in Christ but that such growth continues beyond the grave.

Once again the issue of human freedom crops up: Does God perfect us by sheer power without our cooperation or does he achieve it by love in relation to freedom? On earth God makes us holy not by force but by engaging us in a relationship of mutual responsiveness with himself. The picture which comes to my mind is that of the male and female dancers in a ballet, who support and lead one another on with care and sensitivity. Attaining holiness takes time and cannot be done automatically by superior power. Our Wesleyan and Arminian thinking may need to be extended in this direction. Is a doctrine of purgatory not required by our doctrine of holiness? God does not make us Christlike without our willing it, but as we will it together with him. Grace makes holiness possible, but holiness does not happen unless we receive God's grace and cooperate with it. It seems like we need some space where the gap can be bridged between our imperfect sanctification at death and our perfect life in heaven.

Chapter Four

THE CONDITIONAL VIEW

Clark H. Pinnock

THE CONDITIONAL VIEW

Clark H. Pinnock

THE NATURE OF HELL

The cover story of *US News and World Report* for March 25, 1991, read as follows: "Hell's Sober Comeback. Three out of five Americans now believe in Hades but their views on damnation differ sharply. Theologians are struggling to explain these infernal images." The journalist observed that more people today are taking the reality of hell seriously than in recent years, though they continue to be uncertain about hell's nature; thus a debate around the issue has arisen in the churches. I can identify with that observation. For me too, hell is an unquestioned reality, plainly announced in the biblical witness, but its precise *nature* is problematic.[1]

Of all the articles of theology that have troubled the human conscience over the centuries, I suppose few have caused any greater anxiety than the received interpretation of hell as everlasting conscious punishment in body and soul, an anxiety which is heightened only by the cluster of other dark notions that cling to it in the tradition: I refer to beliefs such as double predestination, the fewness of salvation, and the idea that the

---

[1]For orientation, see G. C. Berkouwer, *The Return of Christ* (Grand Rapids: Eerdmans, 1972), ch. 13; Peter Toon, *Heaven and Hell, A Biblical and Theological Overview* (Nashville: Thomas Nelson, 1986); Dale Moody, *Hope of Glory* (Grand Rapids: Eerdmans, 1964), 94–112; and Harry Blamires, *Knowing the Truth About Heaven and Hell* (Ann Arbor, Mich.: Servant Books, 1988).

plight of the damned brings delight to the saints who behold it from heaven's glory. Even though the focus here is on the nature of hell as everlasting punishment—and there is no space to refute the ideas associated with it, however deserving of refutation—it would be a mistake not to point to the larger pattern to which the traditional view of hell belongs and which accentuates the horror. According to the larger picture, we are asked to believe that God endlessly tortures sinners by the million, sinners who perish because the Father has decided not to elect them to salvation, though he could have done so, and whose torments are supposed to gladden the hearts of believers in heaven. The problems with this doctrine are both extensive and profound.[2]

Not surprisingly, the traditional view of the nature of hell has been a stumbling block for believers and an effective weapon in the hands of skeptics for use against the faith. The situation has become so serious that one scarcely hears hell mentioned at all today, even from pulpits committed to the traditional view. This fact demonstrates that its defenders are not enthusiastic about it, even though the doctrine remains on the books. The Westminster Confession, for example, states that the non-elect "shall be cast into eternal torments and be punished with everlasting destruction" (33.2). Even when an individual does have the stomach to defend the doctrine, there is seldom the delight or pleasure in it as earlier generations had and never any mention of predestination in the presentation. The doctrine once in full flower is drooping.[3]

The purpose of this chapter is to give the rationale for an alternate interpretation of the nature of hell. It is no denial of the reality of hell or the fact that the finally impenitent wicked

---

[2]In defense of the traditional view of the nature of hell, see Robert Morey, *Death and the Afterlife* (Minneapolis: Bethany House, 1984); Anthony A. Hoekema, *The Bible and the Future* (Grand Rapids: Eerdmans, 1979), ch. 19; and William G. T. Shedd, *Dogmatic Theology* (Grand Rapids: Zondervan, 1969, orig. pub. 1894), 2:667–754. A briefer recent defense of "eternal punishment" has been done by Leon Morris in *Evangelical Dictionary of Theology*, edited by Walter Elwell (Grand Rapids: Baker, 1984), 369–70.

[3]The history of the gradual fading of belief in the traditional view makes interesting reading: D. P. Walker, *The Decline of Hell, Seventeenth Century Discussions of Eternal Torment* (Chicago: University of Chicago Press, 1964), and Geoffrey Rowell, *Hell and the Victorians, A Study of the Nineteenth Century Theological Controversies Concerning Eternal Punishment and the Future Life* (Oxford: Clarendon Press, 1974).

will suffer in it, but only a questioning of the traditional theory about its nature. I will argue that it is more scriptural, theologically coherent, and practical to interpret the nature of hell as the destruction rather than the endless torture of the wicked. I will maintain that the ultimate result of rejecting God is self-destruction, closure with God, and absolute death in body, soul, and spirit. I take the verse seriously that says: "The wages of sin is death" (Rom. 6:23). This view does not portray God as being a vindictive and sadistic punisher. Hell is the possibility that human beings may choose in their freedom and thus break relations with God. God loves these persons and does not choose death for them, but hell is nevertheless a possibility arising out of their sin and obduracy. Hell is not the beginning of a new immortal life in torment but the end of a life of rebellion. Hell is, as C. S. Lewis said, the "outer rim where being fades away into nonentity."[4]

It is conceivable that the position I am advancing on the nature of hell is most adequate not only in terms of exegesis and theological, rational coherence, as I hope to prove, but also better in its potential actually to preserve the doctrine of hell for Christian eschatology. For, given the silence attending the traditional view today even among its supporters, the whole idea of hell may be about to disappear unless a better interpretation can be offered about its nature. It seems to me that for many believers today, faced with a choice between hell as everlasting conscious punishment and universal salvation, will choose universalism. What I offer them is a third possibility and another choice. I will try to prove that understanding hell as final destruction proves superior to both the traditional view and its current rival in every way.[5]

---

[4]C. S. Lewis, *The Problem of Pain* (London: Collins, 1957), 115. I am unsure whether Lewis was consistent in his view of the nature of hell; see an earlier essay of mine, "The Destruction of the Finally Impenitent," *Criswell Theological Review* 4 (1990), 243–59.

[5]Evangelical authors who have persuaded me of this position are: John R. W. Stott, in the book he wrote jointly with David Edwards, *Essentials, A Liberal-Evangelical Dialogue* (London: Hodder & Stoughton, 1988), 313–20; Edward Fudge, *The Fire That Consumes* (Fallbrook, Calif: Verdict, 1982); Philip E. Hughes, *The True Image, The Origin and Destiny of Man in Christ* (Grand Rapids: Eerdmans, 1989), 398–407; Stephen Travis, *I Believe in the Second Coming of Christ* (Grand Rapids: Eerdmans, 1982), 196–99; Michael Green, *Evangelism Through the Local Church* (London: Hodder & Stoughton, 1990), 70. Fudge has written the best book and, because it is difficult to find, the address to which one can write to get a copy is: P. O. Box 218026, Houston, TX 77218.

HELL IN THE TRADITION

To engage any theological topic, one joins an ongoing conversation. Therefore, as background to a presentation of my own view of the nature of hell, it is appropriate to conduct a brief review of the standard interpretation in the tradition. Not incidentally, I want to be sure my readers are aware of the full horror of the view I am proposing to revise.[6]

There was no single Jewish view of hell.[7] Many sources present the destruction of the wicked (e.g., Wisd. Sol. 4:18–19; 5:14–15), while others speak of everlasting conscious torment (e.g., 1 Enoch 27:1–3). There is a similar diversity in the early Christian sources. The Apostles' Creed affirms that Jesus will return to judge the living and the dead at the end of history, though it does not spell out the exact nature of that judgment. One can find the idea of everlasting torment (in Tertullian), annihilation (in the *Didache*), and universalism (in Origen).[8]

The diversity was not to last, however. The view of hell as everlasting physical and mental torture came to dominate orthodox thinking early on. Hell as a place of severe torment amidst material flaming fire was to achieve quasi-official status in several texts: for example, "If anyone says that the punishment of devils and wicked men is temporary and will eventually cease, let him be anathema" (Constantinople, A.D. 543). The wicked may expect "perpetual punishment" (The Fourth Lateran, 1215). "If anyone dies unrepentant in the state of mortal sin, he will undoubtedly be tormented forever in the fires of an everlasting hell" (Pope Innocent IV, 1224). And, "If anyone says that the punishments of the damned in hell will not last forever, let him be anathema" (Vatican I, 1870). Such views were immortalized by the poet Dante in *The Inferno*, including the notion that the saints in glory will derive pleasure from contemplating the torments of the damned. Delight in the pains of the lost, though reprehensible to us today, is a logical extension of the doctrine, because (if true) hell would magnify

---

[6]For an exposition of the traditional view, see "Hell" in *The Catholic Encyclopedia*, edited by Charles Herbermann et al. (New York: The Encyclopedia Press, 1913), 7:207–11.

[7]Richard Bauckham, "Early Jewish Visions of Hell," *Journal of Theological Studies* 41 (1990), 355–85.

[8]Jaroslav Pelikan, *The Shape of Death: Life, Death and Immortality in the Early Fathers* (New York: Abingdon, 1961).

God's justice and provide a vivid contrast with the bliss of heaven.

Augustine taught us to view hell as a condition of endless conscious torment in body and soul. In his *The City of God* (Book 21), he defends this view and argues at length against all objections to the notion. In answer to one objection, he muses over how a resurrected body could burn physically and suffer psychologically forever without being materially consumed or losing consciousness. He saw a problem—how could the wicked suffer the sort of burns one would sustain on earth from close contact with raging flames and not be consumed by them? To explain this marvel, Augustine assures us that God has the power to do miracles which transcend ordinary nature and that he will employ this power to keep sinners alive and conscious in the fire. One must suppose that an ancient reader was moved by Augustine's theological acumen, but I doubt that many today are able to receive his remarks.

Nevertheless, the power of Augustine's vision is overwhelming and has dominated the Christian imagination for over a millennium. The Protestant theologian Jonathan Edwards is no less rigorous in his doctrine of hell. His famous sermon, "Sinners in the Hands of an Angry God," paints the image of God dangling sinners over the flames like so many loathsome spiders. "O sinner, you hang by a slender thread, with the flames of divine wrath flashing about it, and ready every moment to singe it, and burn it asunder." Edwards played on human fear to bring souls to God.[9] John Gerstner, a scholar of Edwards, nicely summarizes his view, which he shares:

> Hell is a spiritual and material furnace of fire where its victims are exquisitely tortured in their minds and in their bodies eternally, according to their various capacities, by God, the devils, and damned humans including themselves, in their memories and consciences as well as in their raging, unsatisfied lusts, from which place of death God's saving grace, mercy, and pity are gone forever, never for a moment to return.[10]

---

[9]Jonathan Edwards, *The Works of Jonathan Edwards* (Carlisle, Pa.: Banner of Truth, 1970), 515–25.

[10]John Gerstner, *Jonathan Edwards On Heaven and Hell* (Grand Rapids: Baker, 1980), 53. Gerstner himself has recently published a book on everlasting punishment, entitled *Repent Or Perish* (Ligonier, Pa.: Sola Dei Gloria, 1990), to commend Edwards' position to modern readers because he knows that it has

So it is not only God's pleasure to torture the wicked everlastingly, but it will be the happiness of the saints to see and know that this is being faithfully done. Reading Edwards gives one the impression of people watching a cat trapped in a microwave squirm in agony, while taking delight in it. Thus will the saints in heaven, according to Edwards, consider the torments of the damned with pleasure and satisfaction.

DIFFICULTIES WITH THE TRADITIONAL VIEW

Obviously there are difficulties with this doctrine large enough to encourage theologians to consider revising it. Just ask yourself: How can one reconcile this doctrine with the revelation of God in Jesus Christ? Is he not a God of boundless mercy? How then can we project a deity of such cruelty and vindictiveness? Torturing people without end is not the sort of thing the "Abba" Father of Jesus would do. Would God who tells us to love our enemies be intending to wreak vengeance on his enemies for all eternity? Hans Küng poses a hard question: "What would we think of a human being who satisfied his thirst for revenge so implacably and insatiably?"[11]

But there are so many other problems. What does this tradition do to the moral goodness of God? Torturing people forever is an action easier to associate with Satan than with God, measured by ordinary moral standards and/or by the gospel. And what human crimes could possibly deserve everlasting conscious torture? The traditional view of hell is a very disturbing concept that needs reconsideration.

In a recent book defending the traditional view of the nature of hell, Robert Morey complains that in every generation people keep questioning the orthodox belief in everlasting conscious torment, even though the basis for it has been laid out time and again in books like his. The explanation for this is simple: Given the cruelty attributed to God by the traditional doctrine, it is inevitable that sensitive Christians would always wonder if the doctrine is true.

---

few defenders. Arthur W. Pink was quite as rigorous as Gerstner in *Eternal Punishment* (Swengel, Pa.: Reiner Publications, n.d.).

[11]Hans Küng, *Eternal Life, Life After Death as a Medical, Philosophical, and Theological Problem* (New York: Doubleday, 1984), 136.

ALTERNATIVE INTERPRETATIONS OF HELL

Because of the severe problems that attach to the traditional view, it is natural for alternative interpretations to be proposed. These represent fresh attempts to understand the scriptural data, new paradigms of the nature of hell that need to be tested. This very book is a discussion between viable and influential alternative models for understanding hell.

Metaphor. The most modest revision (and for that reason, the most attractive possibility for those who honor tradition highly) involves reconsidering the nature of the unending pains of hell, taking them in a metaphorical sense. Jean-Paul Sartre shows us how to do this in his play *No Exit.* He asks us to imagine hell as a shabby hotel where three sinners are forever tied to one another in a vicious circle and where each mentally torments, and is tormented by, the others. There is no need for red-hot pokers or burning sulphur because "hell is other people." This is most appealing because it sounds like the traditional view but without any physical suffering, only the intrinsic pain and remorse of a life lived for one's self. For Blamires, "It is only necessary to picture reliving devoid of penitence to guess what the human lot in hell must be like."[12]

This position signifies, in traditional language, that there is the pain of loss but not the pain of sense, the fire being metaphorical. It is a version that sounds traditional without being sadistic or vindictive and hence does not run into the objections mentioned. Augustine and Edwards, of course, would have rejected it as involving softening concessions. They would ask, "Why do you suppose that the fire is not material and will not burn? Are we not raised in body and soul so as to feel its heat?" And, I would add, what is gained if the torment is equally grievous as they insist? If mental suffering is as grievous as physical, how does this help us? It is not the traditional view, but it is no improvement on it either.

Universalism. A second revision stemming from Origen is more radical, turning hell into a purging and refining fire that finally deposits all its inhabitants in heaven. It would abolish eternal torment completely, making hell into a temporary

---

[12]Harry Blamires, *Knowing the Truth About Heaven and Hell*, 76. Others of the British literary evangelicals follow this metaphorical direction: see Charles Williams, *Descent Into Hell* (Grand Rapids: Eerdmans, 1973) and C. S. Lewis, *The Great Divorce* (New York: Macmillan, 1963).

condition of finite and graded punishments, leading to heaven in the end. The sufferings of the wicked in hell would not be endless but would result in the salvation of everyone (universalism). This is an attractive position because it takes sin seriously, while upholding God's unqualified victory. It is also an easy position for traditionalists to switch to, because all it really requires them to do is to expand the number of people elected to salvation. This process presents little problem because within Augustinian logic, it has always been possible to imagine God electing everybody to salvation and effecting his will irresistibly the normal way. Followers of Augustine make excellent universalists, once they accept John 3:16 and 1 Timothy 2:4.[13] Lying behind the logic, Berkhof mentions something more personal: "For God's sake we hope hell will be a form of purification."[14]

There is a slight problem, of course. God may wish to save everybody, but what if someone does not want to be saved? What then? Will God predetermine such a person to love him? That does not make a lot of sense. How can God predestine the free response of love? This is something even God cannot do. All we can say is this: God does not cease to work for the salvation of the world but has to accept the outcome. Hell is proof of how seriously God takes human freedom.[15]

Annihilationism. My own position is a third possibility, called annihilationism or conditional immortality. Being unable to discount the possibility of hell as a final irreversible condition, I am forced to choose between two interpretations of hell: Do the finally impenitent suffer everlasting, conscious punishment (in body and soul, either literally or metaphorically), or do they go out of existence in the second death? In other words, does hellfire torment or consume? I contend that God does not grant immortality to the wicked to inflict endless pain

---

[13]Karl Barth shows the way by his expansion of election to cover all humanity in Jesus Christ: see *Church Dogmatics* (Edinburgh: T. & T. Clark, 1957), 2/2, ch. 7.

[14]Hendrikus Berkhof, *Christian Faith, Introduction to the Study of the Faith* (Grand Rapids: Eerdmans, 1979), 232. For a modern defense of universal salvation, see J. A. T.Robinson, *In the End, God: A Study of the Christian Doctrine of the Last Things* (London: James Clarke, 1950), ch. 9.

[15]John Hick, *Evil and the God of Love*, 379; C. S. Lewis, *The Problem of Pain*, 107; and Stephen T. Davis, "Universalism, Hell, and the Fate of the Ignorant," *Modern Theology* 6 (1990), 173–86.

upon them but will allow them finally to perish. E. G. Selwyn writes:

> There is little in the NT to suggest a state of everlasting punishment, but much to indicate an ultimate destruction or dissolution of those who cannot enter into life: conditional immortality seems to be the doctrine most consonant with the teaching of Scripture.[16]

I know this is not the traditional view of the nature of hell, but I hope that my readers will be willing to entertain the possibility that the tradition has gone wrong in this matter. It is common for evangelicals to say that Augustine and tradition got other things wrong: e.g., the doctrine of the millennium, the practice of infant baptism, and God's sovereign reprobation of the wicked. It should be possible, then, for my readers to entertain the further possibility (for the sake of argument) that he erred about the nature of hell too. Theology sometimes needs reforming; maybe it needs reforming in the matter that lies before us. I believe it does and invite the reader to consider the possibility as a thought experiment.[17]

HELL AS CLOSURE AND ABSOLUTE DEATH

Biblical Interpretation. Evangelical theology starts with the Bible and asks what the Scriptures have to say about the nature of hell. The Bible enjoys primacy relative to other sources for theology, being our canon and teacher. Whatever it teaches about hell we are obliged to accept. So there is no disagreement on that score between traditionalists and my point of view, even though they often try to make an issue of it. The ritual that they follow will be familiar. Traditionalists solemnly confess that their belief in everlasting hellish torment is a genuinely awful concept which appalls them but go on to add that the view is mandatory because Jesus and the Bible teach it, giving them no choice except to believe it. By admitting its unpleas-

---

[16]Edward G. Selwyn, *The First Epistle of St. Peter* (London: Macmillan, 1961), 358.

[17]Annihilationism is not the view of the majority of conservative theologians who accept the traditional view of the nature of hell. In addition to Robert Morey, William Shedd, and John Gerstner already mentioned, see also Anthony A. Hoekema, *The Bible and the Future*, ch. 19; Harry Buis, *The Doctrine of Eternal Punishment* (Philadelphia: Presbyterian and Reformed, 1957); and Millard Erickson, *Christian Theology* (Grand Rapids: Baker, 1985), 1234–40.

antness, they hope to prove their unswerving fidelity to the Bible and a certain heroism in their believing such an awful truth just because Scripture teaches it. They make it sound as if the infallibility of the Bible were at stake.[18] But is it really?

Given the peculiar character of eschatological assertions, modesty in interpretation is surely called for. Biblical texts on our future condition, like those on creation, supply little by way of specific information. The Bible is reserved about giving us details to satisfy our curiosity. A hiddenness hangs over the subject. The Scriptures do not reveal the time or nature of end things. Colorful symbolic imagery is used which cannot be translated into literal description. From the threat of hell, we may not be able to derive precise knowledge about its nature, any more than we can grasp the nature of heaven from the promises God gives us regarding it.

Nevertheless, the Bible does leave us a strong general impression in regard to the nature of hell—the impression of final, irreversible destruction, of closure with God.[19] The language and imagery used by Scripture is so powerful in that direction that it is surprising that more theologians have not picked up on it before now. The Bible uses the language of death and destruction, of ruin and perishing, when it speaks of the fate of the impenitent wicked. It uses the imagery of fire that consumes whatever is thrown into it; linking together images of fire and destruction suggests annihilation. One receives the impression that "eternal punishment" refers to a divine judgment whose results cannot be reversed rather than to the experience of endless torment (i.e., eternal punishing). Although there are many good reasons for questioning the traditional view of the nature of hell, the most important reason is the fact that the Bible does not teach it. Contrary to the loud claims of the traditionalists, it is not a biblical doctrine.

It is a little annoying to be told that no biblical case can be made for the annihilation of the wicked when it is the traditional view that most needs proving. Arthur Pink may call the position on hell as destruction an absurdity, William

---

[18]Let C. S. Lewis speak for the others: "There is no doctrine which I would more willingly remove from Christianity than this, if it lay in my power. But it has the full support of scripture and specially of our Lord's own words" (*Problem of Pain*, 106).

[19]Karl Rahner, *Foundations of Christian Faith, An Introduction to the Idea of Christianity* (New York: Seabury, 1978), 443.

Hendriksen may say that he is aghast that anyone would argue this point, and J. I. Packer may attribute the view to secular sentimentality[20]—but let the reader judge the true situation. The Bible gives a strong impression to any honest reader that hell denotes final destruction, so the burden of proof rests with those who refuse to believe and accept this teaching.

The Old Testament gives us a clear picture of the end of the wicked in terms of destruction and supplies the basic imagery of divine judgment for the New Testament to use. In Psalm 37, for example, we read that the wicked will fade like the grass and wither like the herb (v. 2), that they will be cut off and be no more (vv. 9–10), that they will perish and vanish like smoke (v. 20), and that they will be altogether destroyed (v. 38). One finds the same imagery in an oracle from the prophet Malachi: " 'Surely the day is coming; it will burn like a furnace. All the arrogant and every evildoer will be stubble, and that day that is coming will set them on fire,' says the LORD Almighty. 'Not a root or a branch will be left to them' " (Mal. 4:1–2). While it is true that the point of reference for these warnings in the Old Testament is this-worldly, the basic imagery overwhelmingly denotes destruction and perishing and sets the tone for the New Testament doctrine.

Turning to the New Testament, Jesus' teaching about the eternal destiny of the wicked is bold in its warnings but modest when it comes to precise description. Refraining from creating a clear picture of hell, he did not dwell on the act of damnation or on the torments of the damned (unlike the *Apocalypse of Peter*). Jesus' words on the subject are poised to underline the importance of the decision that needs to be made here and now and not to deal in speculations about the exact nature of heaven and hell. He did not speak of hell in order to convey information about it as a place beyond present human experience and then use that data to press the decision the gospel calls for.

At the same time, Jesus said many things that support the impression that the Old Testament gives of hell as final

---

[20]See Arthur W. Pink, *Eternal Punishment*, 2; William Hendriksen, *The Bible on the Life Hereafter* (Grand Rapids: Baker, 1963), 188; J. I. Packer, "Evangelicals and the Way of Salvation: New Challenges to the Gospel—Universalism and Justification by Faith," in *Evangelical Affirmations*, ed. K. S. Kantzer and Carl F. H. Henry (Grand Rapids: Zondervan, 1990), 126.

destruction. Our Lord spoke plainly of God's judgment as the annihilation of the wicked when he warned about God's ability to destroy body and soul in hell (Matt. 10:28). He was echoing the terms that John the Baptist had used when he pictured the wicked as dry wood about to be thrown into the fire and chaff about to be burned (Matt. 3:10, 12). Jesus warned that the wicked would be cast into hell (Matt. 5:30), like garbage thrown into *gehenna*—an allusion to the valley outside Jerusalem where sacrifices were once offered to Moloch (2 Kings 16:3; 21:6) and where garbage may have smoldered and burned in Jesus' day. The wicked would be burned up just like weeds thrown into the fire (Matt. 13:30, 42, 49–50). Thus the impression Jesus leaves us with is a strong one: The impenitent wicked can expect to be destroyed by the wrath of God.

The apostle Paul creates the same impression when he wrote of the everlasting destruction that would come upon unrepentant sinners (2 Thess. 1:9). He warned that the wicked would reap corruption (Gal. 6:8) and stated that God would destroy the wicked (1 Cor. 3:17; Phil. 1:28); he spoke of their fate as a death that they deserved to die (Rom. 1:32), the wages of their sins (6:23). Concerning the wicked, the apostle stated plainly and concisely: "Their destiny is destruction" (Phil. 3:19). In all these verses, Paul made it clear that hell would mean termination.

It is no different in any other New Testament book. Peter spoke of the "destruction of ungodly men" (2 Peter 3:7) and of false teachers who denied the Lord, thus bringing upon themselves "swift destruction" (2:1, 3). He said that they would be like the cities of Sodom and Gomorrah that were burned to ashes (2:6), and that they would perish like the ancient world perished in the great Flood (3:6–7). The author of Hebrews likewise referred to the wicked who shrank back and would be destroyed (Heb. 10:39). Jude pointed to Sodom as an analogy to God's final judgment, being the city that underwent "the punishment of eternal fire" (Jude 7). Similarly, the apocalypse of John speaks both of a lake of fire that will consume the wicked and of the second death (Rev. 20:14–15). Throughout its pages, following the Old Testament lead, the New Testament employs images of death, perishing, destruction, and corruption to describe the end of the wicked.

A fair person would have to conclude from such texts that the Bible can reasonably be read to teach the final destruction of the wicked. It is shocking to be told that there is no basis for thinking in this way. Clearly it has plausibility as an interpretation and integrity as an opinion. It is a natural interpretation of the basic nature of the divine judgment. I sincerely hope that traditionalists will stop saying that there is no biblical basis for this view when there is such a strong basis for it.

Immortality of the Soul. What then might account for the misreading of the Bible represented by the traditional view of hell? What have our teachers not noticed so that hell connotes something other than destruction? What has created the strong conviction that this destruction language cannot mean what it says?

An explanation for this exists in a hellenistic belief about human nature that has dominated Christian thinking about eschatology almost from the beginning. I refer to the belief in the immortality of the soul which, when accepted, must necessarily skew the exegesis. I believe that the real basis of the traditional view of the nature of hell is not the Bible's talk of the wicked perishing but an unbiblical anthropology that is read into the text. If a biblical reader approached the text with the assumption that souls are naturally immortal, would they not be compelled to interpret texts that speak of the wicked being destroyed to mean that they are tortured forever, since according to that presupposition souls cannot go out of existence? Such a belief, when applied to the biblical texts as an interpretative grid, would have to result in a misreading of the data. If souls are naturally immortal, they must necessarily spend a conscious eternity somewhere and, if there is a *gehenna* of fire, they would have to spend it alive in fiery torment. It is this belief in natural immortality rather than biblical texts that drives the traditional view of the nature of hell as everlasting conscious punishment and prevents people reading the Bible literally.[21]

Belief in the immortality of the soul has long attached itself to Christian theology. There has been a virtual consensus that the soul survives death because it is by nature an incorporeal substance. The assumption goes back to Plato's view of the soul as metaphysically indestructible, a view shared by Augustine,

---

[21]Traditionalists are sometimes very literalistic but not always. For a classic defense of conditionalism, see LeRoy Edwin Froom, *The Conditionalist Faith of our Fathers*, 2 vols. (Washington, D.C.: Review and Herald, 1965).

Aquinas, and Calvin.[22] Jacques Maritain states it for us: "The human soul cannot die. Once it exists, it cannot disappear; it will necessarily exist forever and endure without end."[23] This concept has influenced theology for a long, long time, but it is not biblical.

The Bible does not teach the natural immortality of the soul; it points instead to the resurrection of the body as God's gift to believers.[24] God alone has immortality (1 Tim. 6:16) but graciously grants embodied life to his people (1 Cor. 15:21, 50–54; 2 Tim. 1:10). God gives us life and God takes it away. There is nothing in the nature of the human soul that requires it to live forever. The Bible teaches conditionalism: God created humans mortal with a capacity for life everlasting, but it is not their inherent possession. Immortality is a gift God offers us in the gospel, not an inalienable possession. The soul is not an immortal substance that has to be placed somewhere if it rejects God. If a person does reject God finally, there is nothing in biblical anthropology to contradict what Jesus plainly taught— God will destroy the wicked, body and soul, in hell. Once this is seen, a person is free to read the Bible on hell naturally and straightforwardly.[25]

The Greek doctrine of immortality has affected theology unduly on this point—a good example of the occasional hellenization of Christian doctrine. The idea of souls being naturally immortal, however, distorts the interpretation of biblical texts about hell. It virtually requires a person to stretch the experience of destruction into endless conscious torment. Presumably the traditional view of the nature of hell was originally constructed in the following way: People mixed up

---

[22]See Bruce Reichenbach, *Is Man the Phoenix? A Study of Immortality* (Grand Rapids: Eerdmans, 1983), ch. 7.

[23]Jacques Maritain, *The Range of Reason* (London: Geoffrey Bles, 1953), 60. See John W. Cooper, *Body, Soul and Life Everlasting* (Grand Rapids: Eerdmans, 1989), 17, and Murray J. Harris, *Raised Immortal: Resurrection and Immortality in the New Testament* (Grand Rapids: Eerdmans, 1983), 189–205.

[24]Oscar Cullmann, *Immortality of the Soul or Resurrection of the Body* (London: Epworth, 1958).

[25]Harold O. J. Brown knows this and therefore writes very uncertainly in his defense of the traditional view of the nature of hell: "Will the Lost Suffer Forever?" *Criswell Theological Review* 4 (1990), 261–78. F. F. Bruce admits to conditionalism in the preface to Edward Fudge's book, *The Fire that Consumes*. It is the central argument of Philip Hughes in favor of hell as annihilation in *The True Image*, ch. 37.

their belief in divine judgment after death (which is scriptural) with their belief in the immortality of the soul (which is unscriptural) and concluded (incorrectly) that the nature of hell must be everlasting conscious torment. The logic would be impeccable if only the second premise were not false. Of course, it might be the case that God will still give immortality to the wicked and require them to experience it in everlasting fiery torment. My argument does not rule that out, though it would be a problem explaining why he would choose to do so.

These first two points (the exegesis of Scripture and the unbiblical doctrine of the immortality of all souls) belong together and mutually suggest that the wicked are not going to be tortured forever. The Bible warns against absolute loss in hell and has the anthropological assumption to support that possibility. Orthodoxy needs to straighten out its anthropology.

Morality. The traditional view also runs into deep objections beyond the exegetical. There are moral, judicial, and metaphysical problems to face. Let us begin with the moral problems surrounding the traditional view, which depicts God acting in a way that contradicts his goodness and offends our moral sense.

According to Christian theology the nature of God is revealed in Jesus Christ and shown to be boundlessly merciful. God loves the whole world. His heart is to invite sinners to a festive meal (Matt. 8:11). He is a forgiving and loving Father toward them (Luke 15:11–32), not a cruel and sadistic torturer as the traditional view of hell would suggest. What would the goodness of God mean if God torments people everlastingly? Of course, it is not our place to criticize God, but it is permitted to think about what we are saying. The traditional view of the nature of hell does not cohere well with the character of God disclosed in the gospel; at least, it must make one think twice before concluding that hell spells everlasting conscious punishing.

Our moral intuition agrees with this. There is a powerful moral revulsion against the traditional doctrine of the nature of hell. Everlasting torture is intolerable from a moral point of view because it pictures God acting like a bloodthirsty monster who maintains an everlasting Auschwitz for his enemies whom he does not even allow to die. How can one love a God like that? I suppose one might be afraid of him, but could we love and respect him? Would we want to strive to be like him in this mercilessness? Surely the idea of everlasting conscious torment raises the problem of evil to impossible heights. Antony Flew was right to object that if Christians really believe that God created people with the full intention of torturing some of them in hell forever, they might as well give up the effort to defend Christianity. In that case, the apologetic task in relation to theodicy would be utterly hopeless.[26] John Stott seems to agree: "I find the concept intolerable and do not understand how people can live with it without either cauterizing their feelings or cracking under the strain."[27]

Many attempts have been made to hide the problem. Charles Hodge and B. B. Warfield, for example, lower the population of hell by means of a postmillennial eschatology and the automatic salvation of babies who die in infancy, concluding that very few persons (relatively speaking) will be going to hell anyway. Why worry if only a negligible number, statistically speaking, are going to be tormented everlastingly? At least some traditionalists are aware of problems here and try to deal with them. Unfortunately, according to these doughty Princetonians, millions still get tortured forever even under their generous scenario. We need something better than that.

Another attempt to get around the moral problem is to redefine the nature of everlasting punishment. C. S. Lewis does this when he pictures hell in *The Great Divorce* as almost pleasant, if a little drab. He transforms the lake of fire into the kind of place from which to take day trips into heaven and to which to return in order to meet with the theological society in hell on Thursdays.[28] In such renditions, hell may be nasty and inconvenient but certainly no lake of fire.

Though sympathetic with efforts to take the hell out of hell, I find myself agreeing with genuine traditionalists in objecting to the way in which the biblical warnings are emasculated and the moral problem dealt with, by sheer speculation or fancy footwork rather than through any real exegesis. The biblical warnings appear to spell out a terrible destruction awaiting the impenitent wicked; so, if hell is everlasting torment as traditionalists think, they should not try to weasel out of it. Better that

---

[26]Antony Flew, *God and Philosophy* (London: Hutchinson, 1966), 56–57.

[27]Stott and Edwards, *Essentials*, 314.

[28]In another place, though, Lewis sounds much like an annihilationist. Hell speaks of finality more than duration, he says, and it exists on the outer rim "where being fades away into nonentity" (*The Problem of Pain*, 114–15).

people face up to the horror and call for genuine theological renewal on the point.

Morality makes hell a hard topic to discuss calmly. How can anyone with the milk of human kindness in them contemplate the idea dispassionately when the traditional doctrine is so profoundly disturbing? But, if so, are we being driven by subjectivist feelings that we should suppress? James I. Packer says that he objects to the sense of moral superiority he detects in critics of the traditional view and charges they are driven by secular sentimentalism.[29] This is not altogether helpful, however. If secular sentimentality drives saintly John Stott (the person Packer is referring to), what drives Packer? Is it hardheartedness or a thirst for retribution? Enough of that! The real issue here is God's nature and the conscience, not mere human feelings. Is he the God of boundless mercy or one who tortures souls without end?

Any doctrine of hell needs to pass the moral test, and the version I am advancing can do so. An annihilationist does not have to defend everlasting torture, and one oriented to human freedom does not have to deal with divine predestination to hell. According to my view, God is morally justified in destroying the wicked because he respects their human choices. He will not save them if they do not want to be saved. God wills the salvation of all people (2 Peter 3:9) but will fail to save some of them on account of their human freedom. To affirm hell means accepting human significance. Sinners do not have to be saved and will not be forced to go to heaven. They have a moral "right" to hell.[30] The God who seeks our well-being in fellowship with himself will not force his friendship upon anyone. In the end he will allow us to become what we have chosen.

Justice. The principles of justice also pose a serious problem for the traditional doctrine of the nature of hell because it depicts God acting unjustly. Like morality, it raises questions about God's character and offends our sense of natural justice. Hell as annihilation, on the other hand, does not.

Let readers ask themselves what lifestyle, what set of actions, would deserve the ultimate of penalties—everlasting

---

[29]See Packer, "Evangelicals and the Way of Salvation," 126.
[30]Nicolai Berdyaev, *The Destiny of Man* (New York: Harper, 1960), 266–67.

conscious punishment?[31] It is easy to accept that annihilation might be deserved by those whose lives turned in a definitive No to God, but it is hard to accept hell as everlasting conscious torment with no hope of escape or remittance as a just punishment for anything. It is too heavy a sentence and cannot be successfully defended as a just action on God's part. Sending the wicked to everlasting torment would be to treat persons worse than they could deserve.

Consider it on the basis of an Old Testament standard of justice, the standard of strict equivalence: An eye for an eye and a tooth for a tooth (Exod. 21:24). Did the sinner visit upon God everlasting torment? Did he cause God or his neighbors everlasting pain and loss? Of course not; no human has the power to do such harm. Under the Old Testament standard, no finite set of deeds that individual sinners have done could justify such an infinite sentence. This point stands even without invoking the higher standard from Jesus on this very issue. "You have heard that it was said . . . . But I tell you" (Matt. 5:38–39). Jesus' followers are called to a higher standard of justice in the name of the Lord God, who himself operates on a higher one. The commandment of Moses limited the vengeance of unlimited retaliation, and Jesus limits it still more. Under gospel ethics the traditional view of hell is inconceivable.[32] It would amount to inflicting infinite suffering upon those who have committed finite sins and goes far beyond an eye for an eye and a tooth for a tooth. It would create a serious disproportion between sins committed in time and the resulting suffering experienced forever.

Anselm tried to argue that our sins are worthy of an infinite punishment because they are committed against an infinite majesty. This may have worked in the Middle Ages, but it will not work as an argument today. We do not accept inequality in judgments on the basis of the honor of the victim, as if stealing from a doctor is worse than stealing from a beggar. The fact that we have sinned against an infinite God does not justify an infinite penalty. No judge today would calibrate the degree of punishment on a scale of the honor of the one who

---

[31]On these lines, see Marilyn Adams, "Hell and the God of Justice," *Religious Studies* 11 (1975), 433–47.

[32]See John H. Yoder, "The Political Axioms of the Sermon on the Mount," *Original Revolution* (Scottdale, Pa.: Herald Press, 1971), ch. 2.

has been wronged. The old arguments for hell as everlasting punishing do not work.

What purpose of God would be served by the unending torture of the wicked except those of vengeance and vindictiveness? Such a fate for the wicked would spell endless and totally unredemptive suffering. Here would be punishment just for its own sake. Surely God does not act like that. Even the plagues of Egypt were intended to be redemptive for those who would respond to the warning. Unending torment would be utterly pointless, wasted suffering that could never lead to anything good.

My point is that eternal torment serves no purpose at all and exhibits a vindictiveness totally out of keeping with the love of God revealed in the gospel. Hans Küng is right:

> Even apart from the image of a truly merciless God that contradicts everything we can assume from what Jesus says of the Father of the lost, can we be surprised at a time when retributive punishments without an opportunity of probation are being increasingly abandoned in education and penal justice, that the idea not only of a lifelong, but even eternal punishment of body and soul, seems to many people absolutely monstrous.[33]

In mentioning penology, Küng draws attention to the fact that the ideal of punitive, retributive justice underlies traditional thinking about the nature of hell. Sinners will have to pay back what is owed to the last farthing and beyond. God is the ultimate harsh judge in this way of thinking. No doubt it is feared that, should sinners not have this stick raised against them, they would not be deterred from committing offenses against God and humanity.

Annihilation, on the other hand, makes better sense of hell in terms of justice. If people refuse God's friendship, it would not be right to visit on them a punishment beyond what was deserved, such as everlasting conscious torture would be. What would be just is not to keep totally corrupt people alive forever. God has no obligation to keep such souls alive. Destruction is the obvious fate for them. As long as we do not hold to the

---

[33]Hans Küng, *Eternal Life*, 136–37.

unbiblical doctrine of the immortality of the soul, the extinction and elimination of the wicked is the obviously just solution.[34]

But if so, what about possible degrees of punishment in hell that some texts suggest (Matt. 10:15; Luke 12:47–48)? How could extinction make room for that?[35] I am not exactly sure how to answer that because it requires more detailed knowledge of the precise act of damnation than we have been given. I am sure that it is not beyond God's wisdom to figure about how degrees of punishment might enter into this event. Maybe there will be a period of punishment before oblivion and nonbeing. What there cannot be is what the tradition insists on: excessive punishment.

Metaphysics. A final objection to the traditional doctrine of the nature of hell is cosmological dualism. The doctrine creates a lurking sense of metaphysical disquiet. History ends so badly under the old scenario. In what is supposed to be the victory of Christ, evil and rebellion continue in hell under conditions of burning and torturing. In what is supposed to be a resolution, heaven and hell go on existing alongside each other forever in everlasting cosmological dualism. The New Testament says that God is going to be "all in all" (1 Cor. 15:28) and that God is going to be making "everything new" (Rev. 21:5), but the new creation turns out flawed from day one. John Stott does not think it adds up right, asking: "How can God in any meaningful sense be called 'everything to everybody' while an unspecified number of people still continue in rebellion against him and under his judgment?"[36]

What kind of reconciliation and redemption is it if heaven and hell coexist forever, if evil, suffering, and death all continue to have reality? In the new order how can there be still a segment of unrenewed being, i.e., two kingdoms, one belonging to God and the other to Satan, who reigns at least in hell? It just doesn't sound right. Surely God abolishes all that in the new creation. Surely the biblical picture is that of Jesus completely victorious over sin and death, suffering and Satan, and all those enemies consumed in the lake of fire and second

---

[34]Richard Swinburne, *Responsibility and Atonement* (Oxford: Clarendon, 1989), 180–84.

[35]See Robert L. Reymond, "Dr. John Stott on Hell," *Presbyterian* 16 (1990), 48.

[36]John Stott, *Essentials*, 319.

death. Only if evil, death, devils, and the wicked go into oblivion does history issue in unqualified victory. Victory means that evil is removed and nothing remains but light and love. The traditional theory of everlasting torment means that the shadow of darkness hangs over the new creation forever.

Augustine was not troubled by this duality because of the aesthetic motif in his thinking. The parallelism of heaven and hell, of evil and goodness coexisting, contributed to the complex perfection of the whole in his mind. It was a dimension of the divine artistry and much admired by the saints. The bishop wrote:

> The unjust will burn to some extent so that all the just in the Lord may see the joys that they receive and in those may look upon the punishments which they have evaded, in order that they may realize the more that they are richer in divine grace unto eternity, the more openly they see that those evils are punished unto eternity which they have overcome by his help.[37]

In Augustine's view, believers, far from being disturbed by these hellish torments, would experience satisfaction and admiration on account of them. I acknowledge this view but doubt that more than a handful of people today could assent to this cruel aesthetic.

In conclusion, it makes better sense metaphysically to think of the nature of hell as final destruction and of the dwindling out of existence of the wicked, rather than to posit a disloyal opposition existing eternally alongside God in an unredeemed corner of the new creation.

Examination of Proof Texts. We turn now to the proof texts that are appealed to in support of the doctrine of the nature of hell as everlasting conscious torment. There are only a few of them, but they ought to be reviewed. Can they be fairly interpreted along the lines of annihilation? I think one is entitled to expect that.

1. Regarding those cast into *gehenna*, Jesus says: "Their worm does not die, and the fire is not quenched" (Mark 9:48). Some think that this implies everlasting conscious suffering. But it does not imply it if you go back to the imagery of Isaiah 66:24 from which the phrase is drawn. Here the dead bodies of God's enemies are being eaten by maggots and burned up. The

---

[37] Augustine, *On the Sacraments of the Christian Faith*, 2.18.2.

fire and the worm in this figure are destroying the dead bodies, not tormenting conscious persons. By calling the fire unquench-able, the Bible is saying that the fire is not quenched until the job is finished. The tradition misreads this verse when it sees everlasting suffering in it.[38]

2. In a solemn declaration, Jesus says: "They will go away to eternal punishment but the righteous to eternal life" (Matt. 25:46).[39] I admit that the interpretation of hell as everlasting conscious torment can be found in this verse if one wishes to, especially if the adjective "conscious" is smuggled into the phrase "eternal punishment" (as is common).[40] But there are considerations that line up the meaning with the larger body of evidence. In this text, Jesus does not define the nature either of eternal life or of eternal death. He says there will be two destinies and leaves it there. This perspective gives us the freedom to interpret the saying about hell either as everlasting conscious torment (eternal punishing) or as irreversible destruc-tion (eternal punishment). The text allows for both interpreta-tions because it only teaches the finality of the judgment, not its precise nature.[41] Matt. 25:46 is not a proof text for everlasting conscious punishing.

3. What about the text in the famous parable of the six brothers (Luke 16:23–24), in which Jesus describes a rich man (Dives) suffering in hellish torments? Certainly the figure is there in the midst of much contemporary Jewish imagery and folklore. In a classic reversal-of-fortunes parable, the poor man (Lazarus) is carried by the angels to Abraham's bosom (v. 22). But unless there is a lot of room in the patriarch's lap, the detail seems to be imagery rather than a literal description of what the

---

[38]William L. Lane reads the text through Judith 16:17 and gives the meaning as endless torment; see *Commentary on the Gospel of Mark* (Grand Rapids: Eerdmans, 1974), 349. Judith should not determine the meaning of Isaiah or Mark.

[39]In defense of the authenticity of the logion, see P. H. Bligh, "Eternal Fire, Eternal Punishment, Eternal Life (Mt. 25:41,46)" *Expository Times* 83 (1971), 9–11.

[40]Murray Harris takes it this way in *Raised Immortal*, 182–84, as does Robert H. Gundry, *Matthew, A Commentary on his Literary and Theological Art* (Grand Rapids: Eerdmans, 1982), 516. Gundry writes, "The parallel between eternal punishment and eternal life forestalls any weakening of the former." I beg to differ.

[41]As Colin Brown points out in "Punishment,," *The New International Dictionary of New Testament Theology* (Grand Rapids: Zondervan, 1978), 3:99.

future life will actually be like. In addition, the story refers to *hades* (the intermediate state between death and resurrection), not to *gehenna* (the final end of the wicked), and is not strictly relevant to our subject. Nevertheless, the passage is regularly and unfairly appealed to in traditionalist literature to describe hell, not the intermediate state. The fact is that we cannot deduce from it what the final end of the wicked will be, apart from the issue of its literary genre.[42]

4. A more promising proof text for the traditional view is Revelation 14:9–11, which speaks of those persons who worshiped the beast and received its mark being "tormented with burning sulphur in the presence of the holy angels and of the Lamb." It goes further: "The smoke of their torment rises for ever and ever. There is no rest day or night for those who worship the beast. . . ."[43] This text comes closest in my mind to confirming the traditional view. It would be ironical if the issue came down to the interpretation of a single verse in Revelation, given its uniqueness as a piece of literature. But it may do so because traditionalists, deprived of their substandard proof texts in other books of the Bible, will always resort to this passage, even though in view of the difficult genre of Revelation it does not put them in a very strong position.

Regarding Revelation 14:11, we observe that, while the smoke goes up forever, the text does not say the wicked are tormented forever. It says that they have no relief from their suffering as long as the suffering lasts, but it does not say how long it lasts. As such it could fit hell as annihilation or the traditional view. Before oblivion, there may be a period of suffering, but not unendingly. Besides not teaching the traditional view, the text does not describe the end of history either, which is termed the second death, an image very much in agreement with annihilation (Rev. 20:14).

I take John's primary point throughout Revelation to be that everything that has rebelled against God will be overcome and come to an end. G. B. Caird catches the point: "John believed that, if at the end there should be any who remained

<hr/>

[42]For background on the Jewish imagery used in the parable of Jesus, see I. Howard Marshall, *Commentary on Luke* (Grand Rapids: Eerdmans, 1978), 632–39.

[43]On this theme in Revelation, see Calvin R. Schoonhoven, *The Wrath of Heaven* (Grand Rapids: Eerdmans, 1966).

impervious to the grace and love of God, they would be thrown, with Death and Hades, into the lake of fire which is the second death, i.e., extinction and total oblivion."[44]

Drawing my case to a conclusion, I am contending that the objections to the traditional view of the nature of hell are formidable and that the positive basis for understanding hell as annihilation is stronger than the case for the traditional view. Biblical exegesis, theological reasoning, and practical realities all strongly support the view of hell as annihilation.

COMMENTARY ON THEOLOGICAL METHOD

Theological method is an important factor that comes into play whenever we debate any subject in theology. For our reflections to be profound, we need to pick up on some of these dynamics. Since there are four main sources that are regularly appealed to (Scripture, tradition, reason, and experience), let us run a check of them and see what is going on in this debate.[45]

The Bible. Concerning the Bible as source, there are two elements to watch in relation to its authority and interpretation. First, as to its authority, defenders of the traditional view of the nature of hell will often argue thus: "We dislike this doctrine of everlasting torment, but we have to accept it because the Bible teaches it. Does this not just go to show how highly we regard biblical authority?"[46] They claim that believing in everlasting conscious torment is proof of faith in biblical authority and questioning it is proof of the denial of the Bible. Though this might be true in the case of religious liberals, the reader knows by now that this is irrelevant in the present instance. I share this respect for the authority of the Bible with traditionalists and am only contesting their *interpretation* of an authoritative Bible. This is an issue of biblical hermeneutics, not biblical authority.

In relation to biblical interpretation, a key issue is how to interpret eschatological texts. My impression is that traditional-

---

[44]G. B. Caird, *A Commentary on the Revelation of St. John the Divine* (London: Adam and Charles Black, 1966), 186–87.

[45]On theological method, see J. J. Mueller, *What Are They Saying About Theological Method?* (New York: Paulist Press, 1984), and Donald A. D. Thorson, *The Wesleyan Quadrilateral: Scripture, Tradition, Reason and Experience as a Model of Evangelical Theology* (Grand Rapids: Zondervan, 1990).

[46]For example, Harry Buis, *The Doctrine of Eternal Punishment*, 127, and Robert Morey, *Death and the Afterlife*, 100.

ists selectively over-interpret and over-literalize biblical symbols of the future. (I say selectively because most do not take the biblical language of perishing literally!) Being overly literal is unwise because eschatology is an area of biblical teaching (like creation) that what we know by way of specific factual information is limited.[47] The Bible is reserved about giving detailed information about the nature of heaven or hell; therefore, modesty in interpretation is called for. Jesus' sayings about hell, for example, are addressed more to the conscience than to intellectual curiosity. Details such as the time (Mark 13:32), the circumstances (Acts 1:6–7), and the nature (1 John 3:1) of future events are not given to us.[48] My impression is that the traditional view of hell milks a small number of texts for details to support a theory the that Bible does not teach.

Tradition. Tradition plays a major role in determining people's thinking about hell, so I will devote more space to this factor. Though scriptural support for hell as eternal conscious suffering is weak and objections against it are strong, tradition is a formidable argument for holding the traditional view. I do not feel at all comfortable contradicting the likes of Saint Anselm and John Calvin.

I agree that tradition is a valuable source for theology, though it needs correcting from time to time. The key issue here is whether it needs correcting on this detail of eschatology. Evangelicals are clearly not opposed in principle to changing traditions because they have done so regularly. For example, many of us reject infant baptism, double predestination, and the sacramentalism of the mass, all of which are ancient catholic traditions. Thus evangelicals are not in a position to oppose challenging the old view of the nature of hell just because it is an old tradition.

I think one has to look in other directions to explain evangelical stubbornness on this feature of the tradition. At this point, let me mention one such reason: They fear that a change on this would indicate they are going liberal. Many of them have decided that believing in everlasting conscious torment is a defining characteristic of evangelical belief. In a major

---

[47]See my essay "Climbing out of a Swamp: The Evangelical Struggle to Understand the Creation Texts," *Interpretation* 43 (1989), 143–55.

[48]Karl Rahner, "The Hermeneutics of Eschatological Assertions," *Theological Investigations* (London: Darton, Longman & Todd, 1966), 323–46.

conference in 1989 held to discuss what it means to be evangelical, it was seriously debated whether a person such as John Stott or Philip Hughes, who hold to hell as annihilation, should be considered evangelicals. They can be accepted when sprinkling babies but perhaps not when advocating a revision of the tradition on the nature of hell. The vote to exclude such theologians who hold this opinion failed only narrowly. Obviously, a lot of people are wrestling with the legitimate limits of diversity in evangelicalism.[49]

There is a conundrum here. Why do evangelicals who freely change old traditions in the name of the Bible refuse so adamantly even to consider changing this one? Why do they insist on holding to the old position as stated here: "Hence, beyond the possibility of doubt, the Church expressly teaches the eternity of the pains of hell as a truth of faith which no one can deny or call into question without manifest heresy."[50] There must be some factors other than Scripture or tradition driving the issue, factors that may show up when we review the remaining factors of theological method.

Before moving on, let me defend the option of making a change in the traditional doctrine of the nature of hell. All doctrines undergo a degree of development over time—issues such as Christology and soteriology get taken up at various periods in church history and receive a special stamp from intellectual and social conditions obtaining at the time. A variety of factors in society and thought impact the way in which issues are interpreted. All doctrinal formulations reflect to some extent historical and cultural conditions and have a historical quality to them.[51]

Eschatology is not an exception to this principle but rather

---

[49]See *Christianity Today* (June 16, 1989), 60–62. In the conference volume, John Ankerberg said that it was tantamount to denying the deity of Christ and the atonement to question the traditional view of the nature of hell: see *Evangelical Affirmations*, 139–42. Robert Reymond respects Stott highly but is troubled by the unorthodox nature of this belief of Stott. He hopes he can persuade him to change his mind in his above-mentioned article, "Dr. Stott on Hell." On the theological ferment, James D. Hunter put the cat among the pigeons in *Evangelicalism, The Coming Generation* (Chicago: University of Chicago Press, 1987), ch. 2.

[50]The article on "Hell" in *The Catholic Encyclopedia*, 209.

[51]This is explained by Jeffery Hopper (*Modern Theology II, Reinterpreting Christian Faith for Changing Worlds* [Philadelphia: Fortress, 1987], in a chapter entitled "The Recognition of Historical and Cultural Relativity," 4–31.

exemplifies it, having gone through so many changes over the years. Consider the change from the expectation in the New Testament and early church of the nearness of the second coming of Christ to the delayed expectation of later orthodox theologians in regard to it; from a millennial belief in the early centuries to the belief of Augustine that sees God's rule in the world above and beyond history; from placing the final judgment at the end of history to expecting it at the moment of death; from an emphasis on the gloriously resurrected body to an emphasis on the naturally immortal soul, etc. Eschatology is a doctrine in which interpreters should be careful not to place uncritical confidence in what the tradition has said, since it has undergone several large changes and does not speak with a single voice.[52]

With reference to the evangelical context, I realize that in interpreting hell as annihilation, I am adopting a minority view among evangelicals and placing myself at risk among them. Even though these same people permit dozens of differences to exist among themselves and have made many changes themselves to ancient traditions, somehow to propose this change is still forbidden. One can expect to be told that only heretics or near-heretics would think of denying the doctrine of everlasting conscious punishment and of defending annihilation. It seems that a new criterion of truth has been discovered which says that if Adventists or liberals hold any view, that view must be wrong.[53] Apparently a truth claim can be decided by its associations and does not need to be tested by public criteria in open debate. Such an argument, though useless in intelligent discussion, can be effective with the ignorant who are fooled by such rhetoric. Thus, when a noted evangelical such as John W. Wenham shows himself open to hell as annihilation, it is put down to liberal influences in his publisher (InterVarsity Press) and to poor research on his part for thinking it.[54] The same thing happened to me when *Christianity Today* published my view of hell as annihilation (March 20, 1987); Adrian Rogers,

---

[52]See Stephen Travis, *Christian Hope and the Future* (Downers Grove: InterVarsity Press, 1980); Hans Küng, *Eternal Life*; and John Hick, *Death and Eternal Life* (London: Collins, 1976), 194–98.

[53]Robert Morey, for example, will stoop to talking like this: *Death and the Afterlife*, 199–203.

[54]Morey again, *Death and the Afterlife*, 203.

then president of the Southern Baptist Convention, appealed to it to prove that my theology was going liberal.[55]

But despite such tactics of harassment, the view is gaining ground among evangelicals. John R. W. Stott's public endorsement of it will certainly encourage this trend. In a delicious piece of irony, this is creating a measure of accreditation by association, countering the same tactics used against it. It has become all but impossible to claim that only heretics and near-heretics hold the position, though I am sure some will dismiss Stott's orthodoxy precisely on this ground.

Stott himself expresses anxiety lest he should become a source of division in the community in which he is a renowned leader. He writes:

> I am hesitant to have written these things, partly because I have a great respect for longstanding tradition which claims to be a true interpretation of scripture, and do not lightly set it aside, and partly because the unity of the worldwide evangelical constituency has always meant much to me. But the issue is too important to suppress, and I am grateful to you (David Edwards) for challenging me to declare my present mind. I do not dogmatise about the position to which I have come. I hold it tentatively. But I do plead for frank dialogue among evangelicals on the basis of scripture. I also believe that the ultimate annihilation of the wicked should at least be accepted as a legitimate, biblically founded alternative to their eternal conscious torment.[56]

He is right to feel anxious on this score because he is proposing to change what orthodoxy has claimed about the nature of hell. Some will insist that it is an essential doctrine which Stott should have defended against Edwards. They will agree with William Shedd, who wrote: "The common opinion in the ancient church was, that the future punishment of the impenitent wicked is endless. This was the catholic faith; as much so as belief in the Trinity."[57] As long as evangelicals hold this view, persons suggesting change will have to be viewed as heretics.

In closing, I propose turning the tables on the whole issue of hell in the tradition. Rather than insisting that the view of

---

[55]*The Proceedings of the Conference on Biblical Inerrancy 1987* (Nashville: Broadman, 1987), 106.

[56]Stott, *Essentials*, 319–20.

[57]William G. T. Shedd, *Dogmatic Theology*, 2:667.

hell as everlasting conscious torment remain a defining characteristic of orthodox doctrine, we should be throwing it over. In
fact, the entire set of beliefs surrounding hell, including
unending torture, double predestination, and the delight that
the saints are supposed to feel at the pains of the damned, does
orthodox theology absolutely no good. This set of dismal ideas
should be dumped in the name of credible doctrine. Why
should sound doctrine have such burdens to bear? If we would
clean up our act, it might even be possible to save hell as an
intelligible belief.

Reason. Reason is also a valuable source for theology.
Everyone uses reason in assessing the meaning of texts, in
constructing doctrines, and in striving to understand. As
Anselm said: "Faith seeks understanding."

Reason enters theology on both sides of the debate over
eternal torment versus annihilation. Both sides are trying to
present their position on hell as coherent in the light of God's
nature as just and good. We saw that when we reviewed the
issues around the areas of morality, justice, and metaphysics.
On both sides, reasoning operates in a ministerial way, playing
a role in deciding doctrinal questions. Though it is true that
traditionalists appeal more often to mystery than annihilationists do, perhaps in order to get off the painful hook of some of
the objections, the traditional view can be intelligently defended, and I leave the reader to decide which view is most
reasonable.

Experience and Culture. Experience and culture is a fourth
factor that affects theological judgment, as also appears on both
sides of this debate. A lot of cultural and situational input
enters into the discussion. We may even be on the track of the
most important factor.

One can distinguish at least three such influences on the
traditional side from experience and culture. First, there is the
hellenistic belief in the immortality of the soul. As Swinburne
says, "I suspect that one factor which influenced the Fathers
and scholastics to affirm eternal sensory punishment was their
belief in the natural immortality of the soul."[58] Here is a secular
belief influencing theology. Second, it has been common to use
hell as a moral deterrent. Pusey used the belief as a whip to
keep people in line, and he was not alone in this. The orthodox
often fear what will happen in society if the belief in everlasting

---

[58]Richard Swinburne, *Responsibility and Atonement*, 184.

torment were to decline. Would people not behave without moral restraint and the society devolve into anarchy? For such reasons William Shedd considered no doctrine more important than hell, given the increase of wealth and sinful excess he saw growing in the Western world.[59] His reason for defending it, then, involves a strongly contextual factor. Third, Jonathan Edwards used hell to frighten people into faith, and he is not alone in this either. I have heard people oppose hell as annihilation on the grounds that it isn't frightening enough and would let the wicked off too easily. Everlasting conscious punishment is a huge stick that some people do not want to give up. It has always been used to promote the urgency of missions, and the strongest objection to any revision may well come from missionary agencies.[60]

These three points are powerful and make me wonder whether the true strength of the traditional view of hell does not lie in experience and culture rather than in Scripture, tradition, or reason. If so, the irony would be that the traditionalists are operating in the case of hell out of an essentially liberal methodology that makes primary use of contextual factors in respect to doctrine.[61]

But are annihilationists perhaps in the same situation with the experience-culture factor dominating their view as well? There is some evidence of this. The reader will have detected, for example, strong emotion in my rejection of the traditional view. Obviously, I am rejecting the traditional view of hell in part out of a sense of moral and theological revulsion to it. The idea that a conscious creature should have to undergo physical and mental torture through unending time is profoundly disturbing, and the thought that this is inflicted upon them by divine decree offends my conviction about God's love. This is probably the primary reason why people question the tradition so vehemently in the first place. They are not first of all

---

[59]Shedd, *Dogmatic Theology*, 2:745.

[60]Brian A. Hatcher, "Eternal Punishment and Christian Missions: The Response of the Church Missionary Society to Broad Church Theology," *Anglican Theological Review* 72 (1990), 39–61. Opposition also comes from those same agencies in relation to proposals to broaden the evangelical view of other religions and other needed doctrinal revisions.

[61]For an example of such a liberal methodology, see Delwin Brown's comments in *Theological Crossfire*, by Delwin Brown and Clark Pinnock (Grand Rapids: Zondervan, 1991).

impressed by its lack of a good scriptural basis (that comes later) but are appalled by its awful moral implications. This process shows that along with Scripture, they are drawing on moral intuitions in their theological reflection, just as their opponents are doing in theirs. Both sides clearly draw upon the resources of subjectivity and relevance, though my judgment is that the traditionalists are more affected by it than annihilationists.

CONCLUSION

I conclude that the traditional belief that God makes the wicked suffer in an unending conscious torment in hell is unbiblical, is fostered by a hellenistic view of human nature, is detrimental to the character of God, is defended on essentially pragmatic grounds, and is being rejected by a growing number of biblically faithful, contemporary scholars. I believe that a better case can be made for understanding the nature of hell as termination—better biblically, anthropologically, morally, judicially, and metaphysically.

But whatever hell turns out to be like, it is a very grim prospect. Though annihilationism makes hell less of a torture chamber, it does not lessen its extreme seriousness.[62] After all, to be rejected by God, to miss the purpose for which one was created, to pass into oblivion while others enter into bliss, to enter nonbeing—this will mean weeping and gnashing of teeth. Hell is a terrifying possibility, the possibility of using our freedom to lose God and destroy ourselves. Of course, we do not know who or how many will be damned, because we do not know who will finally say No to God. What we do know is that sinners may finally reject salvation, that absolute loss is something to be reckoned with. I do not think one needs to know more about hell than that.

In the current situation, given the difficulties that attend the traditional view of the nature of hell, I think it is possible that changing our view would be a wise step. Rather than threatening the doctrine of hell, it may actually preserve it. The fact is that the tradition of everlasting conscious torment is

---

[62]Wenham hesitates adopting annihilation for fear that it might be seen as lessening hell's seriousness, though he is open to it (see *The Goodness of God*, 37–39).

causing more and more people today to deny hell altogether and accept universal salvation in order to avoid its sadistic horror; on the other hand, the view of the nature of hell that I am proposing does not involve sadism, though it does retain belief in the biblical category of the second death. In any case, the objections to the traditional view of the nature of hell are so strong and its supports so weak that it is likely soon to be replaced with something else. The real choice is between universalism and annihilationism, and of these two, annihilation is surely the more biblical, because it retains the realism of some people finally saying No to God without turning the notion of hell into a monstrosity.

Response to Clark H. Pinnock

John F. Walvoord

This chapter, written by a recognized scholar, illustrates the problem of interpreting the doctrine of hell. Pinnock's widespread quotations from scholars through the centuries are designed to confirm his opinion. The same problem, however, exists in his article as in all views that fail to do justice to the scriptural account. Does human opinion change a situation? Actually, there either is or is not a future of eternal punishment. Whether we agree with it or not has very little bearing on the issue. The vote against it could be unanimous, and still hell might be a reality. God did not consult us when planning his righteous judgment of the sinful human race. The ultimate question is whether the Bible, which is our only source of information about what happens after death, teaches a doctrine of eternal conscious punishment. The same questions raised in other treatments can be raised here.

Conditional Immortality Challenges the Doctrine of Scriptural Inerrancy. This presentation of conditional immortality raises the question whether the Bible was actually inspired by the Holy Spirit and is verbally inerrant, that is, whether it never expresses as true something that is false. As in the metaphorical view, the common assumption that the Bible bends to the wrong conceptions of punishment that existed in the first century implies that the Holy Spirit was not sovereign in guiding the Scripture and that the writers were not kept from error. The teaching of Christ on the subject of hell is also labeled as a misrepresentation. The great majority of those who hold to conditional immortality of the wicked do not subscribe to the doctrine of scriptural inerrancy.

The Conditional View of Immortality Interprets Prophecy in a Nonliteral Sense. Those few evangelicals who do, on the one hand, affirm the inerrancy of Scripture and, on the other, adopt conditional immortality of the wicked do so on the basis that prophecy cannot be interpreted literally. This view of prophecy is commonly held in the church, as illustrated in those who do not interpret literally the doctrine of the millennium and the events that precede the millennium. Such a view of prophecy, however, is contradicted by the fact that fifty percent of the prophecies of the Bible have already been fulfilled, and fulfilled with meticulous accuracy, thus supporting the concept that prophecy was intended to be interpreted literally. It is contradictory for the same theologians who accept the literalness of the second coming of Christ, as embodied in the creeds of the church, to move to a nonliteral view of the events preceding it and of those following it.

Obviously, if it be assumed without proof that prophecy cannot be interpreted literally, then there is no basis for discussing the subject of hell, for the Scriptures cannot then be taken at their face value. The familiar argument that hell cannot possibly be a place of everlasting fire is derived almost entirely from the fact that this is repugnant to human concepts of God. The more conservative interpretation of hell, as embodied in the metaphorical view, did acknowledge that punishment is real and that hell is eternal, even though it may not be literal fire. When all is said, the question of the literalness of the fire is not the ultimate question. Rather, the ultimate question is whether the wicked suffer after death as a matter of retribution, but without moral restoration.

The Conditional View of Immortality of the Wicked Interprets Passages on Destruction of the Wicked Inaccurately and Ignores Passages which Contradict Their Conclusions Regarding Life After Death. Those passages in Scripture that refer to the destruction of the wicked relate to their physical death, not to the cessation of their existence. The treatment on conditional immortality of the wicked, learned though it is, and supported by many famous scholars, simply ignores the passages which contradict its point of view. The Bible is very plain that the wicked continue living after physical death—as stated, for instance, in Hebrews 9:27–28: "Just as man is destined to die once, and after that to face judgment, so Christ was sacrificed once to take away the sins of many people." The judgment is after death, not at death, which implies existence after the body dies.

The discussion on the conditional view of the immortality of the wicked significantly omits any consideration of Revelation 20:11–15. In this passage two important facts are determined. The first is that the wicked are still in hell at this point in the future. As some of these have been dead for thousands of years, it is obvious that they have been in *hades* without termination of their existence up to this point. It is only then that those in *hades* are cast into the lake of fire. If the wicked had not existed after their death, there would be nobody in *hades* and there would be no future judgment. Any view of hell must take into consideration all the passages on the subject, not just those that are selected in favor of a particular point of view.

The Conditional Immortality of the Wicked Ignores Scriptural Evidence of the Continued Sufferings of the Wicked in the Lake of Fire. A notable instance is revealed in Revelation 20:10, where the devil is cast into the lake of fire—I also discussed this in my critique of the metaphorical view. The millennial kingdom is an established period of time. The beast and the false prophet were thrown into the lake of fire at the beginning of that period (Rev. 19:20); now, a thousand years later, if the millennial kingdom be admitted, they are still in the lake of fire, and they, along with the devil, "will be tormented day and night for ever and ever" (Rev. 20:10). If the Scripture wanted to reveal the unending torment of the wicked, how else could it be stated? Passing these passages by as if they do not exist and offering inadequate evidence that the wicked are destroyed at death undermine the whole concept of the conditional view of the immortality of the wicked and make it an untenable position by anyone who accepts the truth of prophecy in Scripture.

The Fact that Unbelievers Deny Eternal Punishment Does Not Change the Situation. The matter is often brought up that the doctrine of eternal punishment is a major obstacle to people accepting the Christian faith. Such unbelief is understandable, but can we win the lost by denying what the Bible teaches about the future? The Scriptures have a long record of prophecies made, ignored, and not believed, that were ultimately fulfilled. A notable instance is the case of Jeremiah warning the royal family that they should surrender to Babylon and save their lives. In Jeremiah 38:17 the prophet warned King Zedekiah that if the Jews surrendered to the King of Babylon their lives would be spared, the city would not be burned, and his family would live. The prophet continued: "But if you will not surrender to the officers of the king of Babylon, this city will be handed over to the Babylonians and they will burn it down; you yourself will not escape from their hands" (Jer. 38:18). Zedekiah chose to ignore the warning. The result was that the royal family was slaughtered and the city and its beautiful temple destroyed (Jer. 39:6). Zedekiah saw his sons and the nobles of Judah destroyed, and while his own life was spared, his eyes were put out after witnessing these deaths. The Scriptures that follow indicate how the city itself was destroyed. The Bible makes clear that it is possible for people to reject the Bible and its warnings of judgment, but this does not change the outcome. There is a penalty for unbelief. Those who do not accept the doctrine of hell, and who reject salvation, will find out too late that they were wrong.

The Conditional View of the Immortality of the Wicked Ignores the Word "Eternal." Opponents of the view of eternal hell characteristically fail to take note of the word *aionios* in the Greek New Testament, which Greek lexicons with no theological bias define as meaning "eternal." Noted scholars can be quoted that there is no argument on this point. If verbal inspiration extends to the words of Scripture, and if the Scriptures declare that hell is eternal, how can a person upholding conditional immortality of the wicked ignore these facts?

It may be concluded that conditional immortality is wishful thinking by those who want to escape the problem of hell by maintaining it is a doctrine not taught in the Bible. It may also be concluded that the nature of hell, its eternity, and its punishments can only be determined by what the Bible teaches. If what the Bible teaches is inaccurate or false, then one is free to deny eternal punishment. But if the Bible is true here, as in other cases where it deals with subjects beyond human knowledge, the interpreter does not have the freedom to say, "I do not believe what it says," especially when all prophecy that has been fulfilled in history was fulfilled literally. If the Bible is verbally inspired and accurate, and if it is the only revelation we have concerning life after death, we have no alternative to what it reveals—and that is to acknowledge that eternal punishment for the wicked will last forever. No one really knows enough about the future to deny what the Bible teaches.

Response to Clark H. Pinnock

William V. Crockett

Clark Pinnock's defence of annihilationism is interesting and contains many good points. He says, for example, that the doctrine of everlasting punishment has caused great anxiety in the Christian world (certainly true) and may be about to disappear unless a better interpretation can be offered about its nature (probably true). As I pointed out in my chapter, the doctrine of hell has eroded over the years because most pastors and teachers have by their silence abandoned the teaching. If this continues, not many generations will pass before the doctrine will find itself consigned to the theological dustbin, a curio of Christianity's intolerant past.

I also agree that the image of saints delighting in the sufferings of the damned is misguided and might reasonably be equated with sadists watching a cat squirm in a microwave. And this leads to Pinnock's most powerful point—the moral argument. He wonders whether the "Abba" Father of Jesus could torture people without end, and what we would think of someone who acted as vindictively as the doctrine of eternal hell suggests God will act.

Pinnock has put his finger on the issue that bothers evangelicals most about the doctrine of endless conscious punishment—that an eternal punishment for temporal sins seems cruel and unfair. Everything we know has a beginning and an end, and the thought of punishment that never ends not only frightens but mystifies us. We try to imagine an eternity where sinners have no hope, where time is meaningless, and where there is no end to existence, and we wonder how God could perpetuate the lives of lost souls as they wander endlessly in the nether gloom. And so we make up new theology—or at least that is what I think Pinnock and his kind are doing.

Convinced that the doctrine of eternal hell is savage beyond belief, Pinnock ignores the contexts and historical settings of the New Testament, opting (as I said in my chapter) for possible interpretations rather than the more probable. What Pinnock needs to grapple with, but does not, is the historical setting in which Jesus' statements about hell are found. Pinnock overlooks the significant fact that the Pharisees were the largest and most popular Jewish sect in first-century Palestine, and they taught that the soul suffered eternal conscious punishment. So when Jesus talked about the destruction of the wicked in hell and referred to their weeping and suffering, the Pharisaic crowds would have understood him to mean endless suffering, unless he specified that the punishment was annihilation (which of course he never did).

Adding to Pinnock's problem is the consistent testimony of Christians in the first half of the second century. Eternal suffering, not annihilationism, is what they taught. (Pinnock's suggestion that annihilation might be found in the Didache [ca. A.D. 125] has no merit; not once does the document talk about this doctrine.) What Pinnock needs to explain, and again does not, is why the generations immediately after the New Testament period were silent about annihilation. Consistently they wrote about the wicked suffering in eternal hell. Is it not reasonable to suppose that they were teaching what their fathers and grandfathers taught?

Pinnock rails against evangelicals (the vast majority, it turns out) who support the metaphorical view. To hold anything other than the traditional view, he says, takes the hell out of hell and amounts to nothing more than an attempt to weasel out of an uncomfortable doctrine. But to say that the metaphorical view takes the hell out of hell is an emotional trick that begs the question, and I think Pinnock knows that. He starts with the assumption that hell must be interpreted as a literal fire and that any change from that takes the hell out of hell. On this reckoning, Jude takes the hell out of hell because in verses 7 and 13 he talks about hell as being both eternal fire and the blackest darkness—clearly metaphorical expressions, as I argued. Jesus also takes the hell out of hell because he uses opposing images of fire and darkness to describe the final place of retribution. The truth is that these incompatible images were never intended to be literal, but were metaphors to describe the awful place we call hell. You cannot take the hell out of hell if the hell you describe is true to the intentions of the biblical authors. If Pinnock objects to the metaphorical view, he must do so by showing why the metaphors should be understood as literal expressions, not by throwing out clichés for emotive effect.

Of course, Pinnock's motivation for rejecting the metaphorical view is clear. He wants to force people to choose between a hell of fire and smoke and annihilationism. But that is not the choice, as I have shown. Throughout Jewish and Greek writings, including the New Testament, fire is commonly used in a nonliteral way to describe God's judgment. It is colorful language that makes a point. Hell should be pictured as a grievous place of unspecified, eternal judgment—perhaps banishment from God—not a burning pit where lost souls writhe and shriek.

But if hell is so grievous, says Pinnock, what is the advantage in supposing it is some kind of mental anguish rather than a literal fire? The metaphorical view is no improvement on the traditional view. This is a specious argument. At issue is not whether one view improves on the other, but which one is correct. I do concede Pinnock's point, however, that sometimes mental suffering can be as arduous as physical, and if this were true for hell, then a metaphorical hell would be as bad as a literal one. I suppose if evangelicals were to search their hearts, they would probably have a deep-seated uneasiness with the doctrine of hell, and the metaphorical language allows them the hope that hell might not be as awful as it appears. In many ways they sense with David that God is often more merciful than we humans: "Let us fall into the hands of the LORD, for his mercy is great; but do not let me fall into the hands of men" (2 Sam. 24:14).

This being said, the metaphorical view does improve on the traditional view in two ways. First, it more accurately represents the intention of the biblical writers. I already have shown that the Jewish and Greek descriptions of hell were not intended to be literal. Second, when Christians feel constrained to teach a literal hell of burning fire, they usually hold their tongues and say nothing about the fate of the lost (as the latter part of the twentieth century testifies). But if they understood that the literal view makes the Bible say too much, perhaps they would be less embarrassed to preach what Jesus so often talked about—the impending judgment of God.

Admittedly, even when we understand hell correctly, it is not a vast "improvement" on the traditional view. Those who reject God still suffer an awful penalty—a penalty that none of us can fully understand. From our perspective, trapped as we are in our finite states, we cannot grasp the awful nature of sin, and consequently we wish that the eternal penalty so clearly enunciated in Holy Writ were otherwise. But the Scriptures must be our guide, not some amorphous hope born of our own desires.

Pinnock ridicules this kind of response, calling it a familiar ritual designed to show how dedicated the believer is to the Word of God. In Pinnock's experience, evangelicals who affirm the doctrine of hell while proclaiming their uneasiness with it are disingenuous; they want to be seen as standing tall for the Word. This has not been my experience; and though I can imagine there are people like that out there, I find his characterization a bit cynical. Most evangelicals, it seems to me, affirm the doctrine of hell almost grudgingly. Why? Because they have a mother or neighbor or friend who has died without embracing Christ, and the possibility of hell for such loved ones genuinely bothers them.

Too often we tend to be swayed by our emotions, by what we wish were the case, and Pinnock's chapter is littered with emotionally charged arguments designed to sweep the reader away from historical, biblical moorings. Emotional arguments can be persuasive (I confess I have not been above using them in my own chapter), but we do not derive our doctrine from them. Nor do we derive doctrine from a collection of *possible* meanings. Rather, we examine the words of Jesus and the apostles in light of the first-century setting and then ask: What would this writer or speaker have meant, given what we know about his audience in the first century? This, Pinnock has not done.

Response to Clark H. Pinnock

Zachary J. Hayes

Professor Pinnock offers a formidable argument for what must be called a minority opinion in the history of Christian theology. Between the possibility of an everlasting, subjective existence of the lost in a state of conscious punishment and the possibility of the eventual salvation of all human beings, Pinnock argues persuasively for the possibility that hell be taken not as a perpetual state of conscious suffering but as the total, irrevocable death of annihilation.

As with the essay of Professor Crockett, so also in this instance, I find the citing of historical antecedents interesting, particularly since my own field of study has been the history of Christian thought. When one has worked in that field for a long time, one begins to wonder whether it is possible to come up with any truly original ideas after some twenty centuries of Christian reflection on the message of the Scriptures.

This presentation of annihilation, unlike others, has certain affinities with major Roman Catholic positions at the present time. I know of no Roman Catholic theologians who hold that the lost are, in fact, annihilated. But when Pinnock argues that such annihilation amounts to a self-destruction brought about not as a punishment from outside God, but that it is the internal working out of the sinner's own stubborn resistance to God, his argument parallels Karl Rahner's understanding of hell as the intrinsic effect of the free choices of human persons. For Rahner, of course, the possibility of hell as a permanent condition remains. But it is seen as a possibility and not

176 I   **Four Views on Hell**

necessarily as a fact. As a possibility, hell is the final extrapola-
tion of Rahner's understanding of freedom. For him, freedom
means not the ability to change our choices endlessly, but the
ability to make choices that have eternal significance. In this
view, God is seen not as a heartless, vindictive judge, but as a
God who takes human freedom so seriously that free human
actions are never bypassed in God's dealings with the world.
We are free and responsible for our actions, and we must live
with the results of our free choices.

Where Rahner and other Catholics differ with Pinnock
would be in Pinnock's conclusion that the final result of our free
choices might be utter self-destruction, that is, simple nonexistence. Rather than make that conclusion, Rahner maintains a
consistently dialectical position. We cannot know the outcome
of history, for how things eventually work out is a matter of
how free human agents respond to the free grace of God. But
because of what God has already done in Christ, we can
maintain the hope of universal salvation together with the
possibility of hell. In the end, however, we cannot claim to
know the outcome of history. That remains an object of hope.
The distinction between knowing and hoping is crucial here.

How do such theologians deal with the texts of the
medieval councils and the words of Vatican Council I cited by
Pinnock? Many leading Roman Catholics see these texts not as
affirmations of the actual existence of hell, but as conditional
statements. That is, if anyone is truly lost, such final loss is a
situation that will last without end. But at no time have any of
the councils ever claimed that a particular human being has, in
fact, been lost. While many Christians may be ready to consign
others to eternal damnation, particularly those with whom they
do not agree or from whom they have suffered injustices, they
ought to recognize their own human propensities in this and
not be too swift to apply such inclinations to God.

It seems to me, then, that a theologian standing firmly in
the Roman Catholic tradition of theology can feel quite
comfortable with the major lines of Pinnock's argument. Such
theologians, and I include myself among them, agree that a
crucial element in the theological doctrine of hell is the
understanding of the seriousness of human freedom. Hell is
something we can do to ourselves! We need not think of God as
imposing a terrible punishment on sinners from the outside.
The question of hell, then, is not: How can a God of love do
such a thing to creatures? Rather, the question is: How

seriously do we take our own God-given freedom? God is involved in hell in the following sense. He has created us for the purpose of eternally sharing in the richness of the divine life of love. The condition for such sharing in love is freedom. But since love cannot be coerced and be truly love, the condition for realizing God's aim is freedom. But if we are dealing truly with genuine freedom, this must include the possibility of the creature rejecting love. Thus the condition for the reality of heaven is simultaneously the condition for the possibility of hell. God need not be thought of as positively willing people into hell. He is involved in the sense that the divine action of grace does not override the reality of human freedom, and such freedom can end in total loss. Whether or not in the light of that loss God withdraws the divine creative power that holds creatures in existence is the basic point at which Pinnock's position differs from that of Rahner and other Catholic theologians.

The question, then, is: Is such final loss simple nonexistence? Or is it a continued subjective existence in the self-enclosed isolation one has chosen in one's historical existence? Annihilationism, as Pinnock presents it, has the aesthetic advantage of allowing us to envision the final condition as a state of total harmony. The other option, lying between universalism and annihilationism, makes it impossible to resolve the dialectical relation between good and evil in a satisfactory way. Even a coincidence-of-opposites model would not seem very satisfactory here. The final coincidence-of-opposites, I would like to think, is that of the relation between God and creation, not the coincidence of a relation between an eternal good and an eternal evil.

I find it interesting that Pinnock's concluding statement could have been written by many a Roman Catholic theologian. The latter would differ from Pinnock only in their interpretation of the phrase to "destroy themselves." But the summary statement, I believe, moves to the central issue of the doctrinal tradition. And I am in full agreement with the suggestion that one needs to know nothing more about hell except that we must reckon with the possibility of final and total loss because of our ability to say No to God.

Perhaps, then, the important thing is that we learn not to place too much weight on particular theological formulations. Certainly we need to reflect on the meaning of Scripture. But if, as we believe, the Scriptures communicate something of the saving mystery of God, we should never fall into the trap of thinking we can ever truly know and understand that mystery. Finally, our theologizing about the meaning of the Scriptures is an effort not to resolve the divine mystery, but to come to a deeper understanding of what it means to trust in the infinite mystery of God's indiscriminate, life-giving, saving love. That this love has been victorious in the case of Jesus Christ is the foundational rock of Christian eschatology on which we can hope to build a life of positive meaning.

In the light of that foundational mystery, we ought not claim to know too much in detail. But we are left with an important question. Can we live with a radical trust in God even as we move through life with vast areas of ignorance? Perhaps this, in the end, is the true meaning of being a person of faith. And perhaps this is one of the most important lessons to be taken from these discussions of eschatological mysteries. There is a great difference between trusting a personal, loving God, and having a foolproof security system. Similarly, there is a vast difference between hoping and knowing. Can we live responsibly in trust and hope without having a clear, detailed knowledge of what awaits us as our future, in this world or in the next?

GENERAL INDEX

Abraham 15, 28, 71, 156
Abyss, fiery, 54, 59
Ad, 23
Adam, 61, 94, 124
Adventists, 86, 161
Ainigma, 57
Aion, 24, 26
Aionios 23–26, 75, 170
Alam, 23
Allegorical interpretation, 83, 102, 119
Amillennial view of prophecy, 78
Analogy, 82–84, 86
Angels, 21–22, 30, 58, 61, 64, 72, 75, 80, 157
Annihilation, 13, 23, 34, 61, 64, 67
  in the *Didache*, 138
  and justice, 153–54
  view of, 135–78
  See also Conditional immortality
Annihilationism, 62, 76, 142
  and harmony, 63
  and gradation of punishment, 73–74
Annihilationists, 66, 68, 71–72, 75
Anselm, 152, 159, 163
Apocalypse of Peter, 66, 145
Apocalyptic literature, 22
Apocryphal writings, 50, 119
Apostle's Creed, the, 138
Apostolic Fathers, 65–66
Aquinas, Thomas, 148
Arminian, 127
Augustine, 37, 46, 85–86, 91–92, 96–97, 105–6, 115, 139, 141–43, 147, 155, 161
Authority of the Bible, 158

Balaam, 16
Barclay, William, 130
Beast, the, 22–23, 26, 47, 75, 80, 157, 169
Berdyaev, Nicolai, 128

Bible, the
  on eternal punishment, 13, 27
  and the church, 109
  inerrancy of, 38–39
  ways of approaching, 102
  as source, 158
  teachings of, 14, 23
  See also Scripture
Blamires, Harry, 141
Buis, Harry, 23–24, 27

Caesar of Arles, 106
Caird, G. B., 157
Calvin, John, 44, 46, 48, 82, 87, 148, 159
Canaan, 25
Carthartic punishments, 113
Catholic Church, *See* Roman Catholic Church
Celsus, 50
Chernobyl, 36
Christ, *See* Jesus Christ
Christ and Time, 34
Christadelphians, 62
Christian literature, 46
Christian theologians, 13
Christianity Today, 45, 161
Christians, early, 66, 138
Christology, 160
Chrysostom, John, 112
Church, the 95, 101, 160
  authority of, 119
  as an organism, 109
  and purgatory, 126
  tradition of 102–4
  See also Roman Catholic Church
The City of God, 139
Clement of Alexandria, 100–101
Coleman-Norton, Paul, 60
Communion of the saints, 98, 112, 118, 124

INDEX OF SCRIPTURE AND OTHER WRITINGS

187